For Joanne

The Great Camaro

by Michael Lamm

Fifth printing, Oct. 1981

©Copyright 1978-81

Lamm-Morada Publishing Co., Inc.
Post Office Box 7607
Stockton, California 95207

Library of Congress catalogue number 78-61758
ISBN O-932128-OO-9

CONTENTS

Chapter One

Green Light for

GENERAL MOTORS found itself in a bit of a pickle when the Mustang hit the road in Apr. 1964. Chevrolet designers were just then putting the finishing touches on a totally reskinned and considerably re-engineered 1965 Corvair.

The corporation hoped at first that this new Corvair for 1965, with its 4-wheel independent suspension and turbocharged aluminum rear engine, could hold the line against the Mustang.

There was no reason at first for GM to doubt that buyers would prefer the 1965 Corvair to the 1964½ Mustang. The Mustang, after all, was essentially a rebodied Falcon, while the Corvair was an entirely separate, distinct car with sophisticated engineering and clean styling.

With this in mind, it's not hard to see why General Motors decided to take a wait-and-see policy toward the Mustang through the summer of 1964. Chevrolet already had five different car lines in the marketplace and didn't relish doing a sixth to bump heads with the Mustang. So as it turned out, 27 months would pass before Chevrolet delivered its definitive Mustang rival, and by that time Ford had sold some 1.3 million Mustangs.

But in Aug. 1964, when Mustang production hit 100,000, GM made the decision to go ahead with an entirely new program aimed at countering Ford's runaway bestseller. Chevrolet called it the F-Car program at first, the purpose being to develop a vehicle for the 1967 model year that could compete head-on with the Mustang—in ways the Corvair couldn't.

As an aside, Corvair sales did take a slight upturn during 1965. This was before November of that year, though, because Ralph Nader published his article *The Corvair Story* in the November issue of *The Nation*. Immediately afterward, his book *Unsafe at Any Speed* was released. A congressional investigation followed, along with lawsuits and attendant adverse publicity, and it was obvious then that GM had made the right decision in instituting the F-Car program.

IT TOOK THE MUSTANG to shake loose the Camaro, but GM designers had been toying with front-engined ponycars long before editor Jim Hamilton coined that term in CAR LIFE.

According to Pontiac chief designer Bill Porter: "As early as 1958, I remember a 4-passenger, sporty-type car of the general size and weight class of the Mustang being worked on in an advanced studio. In the early 1960's, a number of similar cars were developed from time to time, again in the advanced studios. Everyone *wanted* to do one, but at the time there was really no corporate interest . . . ."

Irvin W. (Irv) Rybicki, GM's design vice president, recalls the early beginnings. "I'd say perhaps a year before the first Mustang was introduced, we had the Buick Riviera out on the street. This was the 4-place Riv, and it was selling well.

"I was associated with the Chevrolet studio at the time and, along with some other designers in the room, we got to brainstorming the idea that if the Riviera could do *that* well, at *that price*, what could Chevrolet do with a little 4-place personalized car aimed at a market somewhere around $2500?

"I talked with Bill [William L.] Mitchell about it, and he didn't think it was a bad idea. So we went over into a warehouse on the other side of 12-Mile Road—I took some modelers and designers over there with me—and started a program. I think it was about four months later, we completed the car we wanted. It was a good-looking automobile. I can remember Bill and me going over to the warehouse, and he was as excited about the car as I was."

This all happened, of course, before any green lights were given on the F-Car and, as Mr. Rybicki points out, even before the Mustang made its debut.

Irv Rybicki continues: "We then got Bunkie [Semon E.] Knudsen, who was Chevrolet's general manager at the time, to take a look, and Bunkie said, 'I've got to admit that it's a damned good-looking car, but I'll tell you what Chevrolet doesn't need at the moment and that's another automobile.' At that time we had the Big Chevy, Corvair, the Corvette, the Chevy II, and we'd just put the Chevelle into production—five different nameplates.

"Well, about 10 months later, Ford introduces the Mustang. Nobody paid that much attention to the car until it got up into the 100,000 [sales] range, and then it shook a lot of people, and off we went into designing the Camaro for Chevrolet."

FORD AND GENERAL MOTORS had both been building dreamcars for years to test public reaction. GM's Motoramas of the 1950's and early '60's had put forth several 4-seaters. Ford introduced the Mustang I, a 2-place car with an aluminum body and midship-mounted V-4, in Dec. 1962, then followed it up with the Allegro, Cougar II, and Mustang II showcar series.

The idea in all cases had been to let product planners and researchers test public reaction to certain shapes, lines, concepts, body configurations, and accessories. An autoshow audience could *see* what the car companies were able to offer and thus could, in a sense, vote on or react to specific ideas for future products.

In early 1964, at the New York Auto Show and just a few weeks ahead of the production Mustang's debut on Apr. 17, 1964 at the World's Fair, Chevrolet unveiled a styling exercise based on the Chevy II and called the Super Nova. The Super Nova would be significant, partly because Chevrolet general manager Bunkie Knudsen was on hand for its debut.

"We had done this special little coupe that was pretty cute," Mr. Knudsen said in a recent telephone interview, "and we showed it down at the New York Show—the Super Nova. Pretty little car. When Ford saw it there on the stand, some of their people came over and were very interested. They asked me if we were planning to build it. I told them we would if we could.

"Well, I couldn't get approval. The corporate people wouldn't give us approval. As soon as the Mustang came out, I knew we needed something to compete with it, but we still just couldn't get approval."

When asked whether the restyled Corvair had been a factor in delaying development of the Camaro, Mr. Knudsen answered, "Yes, I would say that the Corvair did have an

the F-Car

Camaro's forebear, the Super Nova made its initial appearance at the New York autoshow a few
weeks before Mustang's introduction in Apr. 1964. Ford representatives asked
Chevrolet general manager Bunkie Knudsen whether the Super Nova was intended for production.
Knudsen said he hoped to build the car but couldn't get GM management approval.

Chevrolet came up with a number of sporty Super Nova variants even before General Motors gave its go-ahead for the F-Car (Camaro) program in Aug. 1964.

effect. As I think back, I feel the Corvair might have been in the minds of those people who refused to let us go ahead with the Super Nova or something *like* the Super Nova.

"I believe they felt—although I didn't—that the new 1965 Corvair, with its reworked suspension and body, would take care of the Mustang. I didn't feel it would, because I was pretty sure the Mustang had a lot more flexibility engineered into it than the Corvair ever would have."

Adds former GM design vice president William L. Mitchell: "What killed the Corvair was that the engine couldn't go any bigger. In those days, throwing gravel was a national pastime; a major sport. You know, kids wanted something that would really take off. No way would the Corvair do *that*. And so Chevrolet went to a car you could put different engines in—different horsepower ratings, different combinations. And you had to go to a front engine to do that."

YOU'VE PROBABLY HEARD it said that the Camaro started life as a dolled-up version of the Chevy II. That's true in a sense, but strictly speaking it's not, because the Camaro came out as a brand-new design for 1967, **but engineered in conjunction with an equally new Chevy II for 1968.** Now this is an important point—one that's not generally recognized. The 1967 Camaro was *not* an adaptation of any existing car, particularly not of the existing Chevy II—not at all the way the Mustang had been an adaptation of the Ford Falcon.

Rather, the 1967 Camaro was engineered and developed from the ground up, together with the totally new Chevy II that came out for 1968.

Most of the same people worked on both cars at basically the same time. The two cars were developed together—jointly. But the Camaro got primary emphasis, appeared first, and was introduced as a 1967 model. The all-new Chevy II waited one year—until 1968—to be introduced. These two cars did, as we'll see, share a good many components in their chassis and running gear.

The decision to go ahead with an F-Car (Camaro) that would lead into a new X-Car (Chevy II) came from the very upper reaches of General Motors and Chevrolet management: the GM executive committee, engineering policy committee, and divisional groups. These committees were influenced largely by men like Edward N. Cole, GM's car and truck vice president at the time, who'd fathered the Corvair and who would soon become GM president; also by Chevrolet's Bunkie Knudsen, who was very much in favor of the F-Car.

Once that decision had been made, though, the job of formulating the Camaro package—its dimensions, performance characteristics, flavor, and marketing direction—had to come about through the combined efforts of Chevrolet, Fisher Body, and GM engineers, designers, planners, and sales people.

The thought was put forth at the beginning that the F-Car should beat the 1967 Mustang in all possible ways. It should handle better, perform better, ride more smoothly, and be just a hair bigger in most dimensions. Chevrolet's chief engineer, Ellis John (Jim) Premo, had primary responsibility for drawing up the F-Car's specifications. Comparing them with the 1967 Mustang, we find the following:

	1967 Mustang	GM F-Car
Wheelbase	108.0 in.	108.1 in.
Overall length	183.6 in.	184.6 in.
Overall width	70.9 in.	72.5 in.
Overall height	51.6 in.	51.0 in.
Front/rear tread	58.0/58.0 in.	59.0/58.9 in.
Front shoulder room	53.4 in.	56.7 in.
Front hip room	53.9 in.	56.3 in.
Front head room	37.4 in.	37.0 in.
Front leg room	41.8 in.	41.8 in.
Rear hip room	50.9 in.	54.5 in.
Rear head room	37.4 in.	36.7 in.
Rear leg room	28.8 in.	30.5 in.
Trunk capacity	9.0 cu. ft.	8.3 cu. ft.
Base 6-cyl. engine	200 cid, 120 bhp	230 cid, 140 bhp
Base V-8 engine	289 cid, 200 bhp	327 cid, 210 bhp
Top-rated engine	390 cid, 335 bhp	396 cid, 325 bhp
Curb weight	2696 lb.	2900 lb.

These were all target dimensions, although most of them stuck. By the end of 1967, the Camaro's top-rated engine would be a 375-bhp version of the 396, with the Z-28 302 putting out nearer 400 bhp.

JUST AS IMPORTANT as the F-Car's dimensions was the way GM planned to fit it into the market. The Mustang had taken a smart direction, and the Camaro, quite frankly, was about to follow.

Ford's marketing strategy had been to offer a basic, sporty-looking car, sell it for as little as possible, then make a long list of options available so buyers could tailor the car to their needs.

Other characteristics set for the F-Car in 1964 and expressed by assistant chief engineer Donald H. McPherson included:

1) Four-passenger packaging in a low-silhouette vehicle, where driveshaft tunnel height wouldn't severely restrict seating and comfort.

2) The use of conventionally arranged and readily available Chevrolet engines from the current family of powerplants.

3) Drivetrains to include 3- and 4-speed manual transmissions plus 2- and 3-speed automatics with both column and floormounted shift controls.

4) One-piece driving rear axles with a full complement of ratios from economy to performance combinations.

5) Conventional but compatible chassis design that would have sharply defined, sports-car-like roadability and maneuverability plus a superior ride and silence through improved road, engine, and driveline isolation.

6) A full range of optional convenience and comfort equipment plus a full range of interior and exterior decor packages.

Camaro picked up Super Nova's console and central instrument panel theme, but practicality dictated tilting the gauge cluster inward and cutting off the console before it reached the rear seat. Henry Haga's studio used the Super Nova as inspiration and a jumping-off point in designing the Camaro.

Chapter Two

Engineering the

THE NEW F-CAR GREW initially from the joint efforts of Chevrolet designers working very closely with Chevy engineers inside GM Design Staff. Later, Fisher Body Div. engineers also became involved.

If we trace the Camaro's early development, we see immediately that Chevrolet Engineering and Chevrolet Design people labored hand-in-hand from the beginning. To understand the F-Car's birth as it actually took place, we note the two functions—engineering and styling—very much intermingled.

But for the sake of this narrative and to simplify our explanation, it's more practical to separate the F-Car's engineering development from its design (or styling) evolution and look at each in turn.

We'll talk first about engineering.

As mentioned, the 1967 Camaro was engineered so it would lend itself to becoming the 1968 Chevy II. That was one of the important "givens" handed down by top GM and Chevrolet management. The 1967 F-Car would form the rootstock for the 1968 X-Car. But to understand the background for the decision to go to a *semi-unitized body structure* for both these vehicles, we have to look at the first (1962) Chevy II and see how GM body engineers profited from past experience.

"The first Chevy II originally came out for 1962," explains former Chevrolet research-and-development (R&D) engineer James G. Musser, Jr., who later became very involved in the Camaro's racing successes. "Frankly, the 1962 Chevy II was patterned pretty directly after the Ford Falcon. It had a fully unitized body structure similar to the Falcon's.

"The initial Chevy II's front suspension, too, used the same arrangement as the Falcon—coil springs *above* the control arms. And copying the Falcon's unit construction resulted in a fairly harsh ride. There was a lot of friction in that front suspension, plus a lack of isolation between the front suspension and body structure. These facts left both the Falcon and the first-generation Chevy II harsh vehicles, with lots of road noise and so forth.

"We concluded that to clean up the 1967-68 Camaro/Chevy II, some redesigning would be necessary. We elected to go with a more conventional front suspension, the general configuration of which we borrowed from the Chevelle. It had the coils *between* the control arms instead of above them. And perhaps most important, we decided to go with a bolt-on subframe up front to carry the front suspension and engine. This subframe would be heavily bushed in rubber to isolate it from the unitized rear body section. We calculated this would smooth out both these new cars considerably."

THE IDEA OF A SUBFRAME wasn't new, but its application to an inexpensive American car like the F/X-Car was.

"The decision to put a subframe under the new Camaro and Chevy II Nova was a compromise between the old, fully unitized Chevy II construction and the use of a full frame," comments then-assistant chief engineer Donald H. McPherson, who later became head of GM's Canadian operations. "I think it was basically a question of,

'How can we build a car for the low end of the market that's got a little more silkiness and isolation than the previous Chevy II?'"

And according to Edward L. Nash, an assistant staff chassis engineer, "We knew that the early Chevy II's bolted-to-dash approach was noisy and harsh. It was also a hard design in which to incorporate rubber mounts.

"The subframe idea was Charlie Rubly's and mine—to prepare a subframe design much like the front part of a conventional full-length frame. We could then easily provide space for rubber mounts, and we tested our Phase I cars with and without rubber mounts. The results with rubber were so good that the only remaining question was how big the rubber biscuits had to go to do the job and yet be durable.

"Wes McCollum was the development engineer, and he instrumented each mount location with triaxial strain-gauged blocks. The peak forces recorded on proving grounds test roads determined the necessary compressive (axial) and lateral (radial) mount capacities. We then chose the proper rubber durometers, and with very good results to date."

Another reason for not going with a full-length frame—besides the cost and

1967 Camaro Development Chronology

Chevrolet F-Car program gets GM management go-ahead.	8/8/64
Preliminary engineering specifications completed.	8/25/64
Styling begins.	8/26/64
Pre-test vehicles assembled from cobbled Chevy II's.	9/64
Sheetmetal styling resolved.	12/64
Bumpers, grilles, lamps okayed.	8/17/65
Instrument panels finalized.	9/19/65
Exterior ornamentation basically finalized.	9/30/65
Sheetmetal tooling done.	11/14/65
Handbuilt prototype Job #1 completed.	12/16/65
Engineering paperwork finished.	1/13/66
Purchase orders completed.	2/24/66
Last prototype sample car received.	5/5/66
Sample approval completed.	6/2/66
Pilot assembly begins.	5/17/66 through 6/5/66
Startup of volume assembly.	8/7/66
Camaros in dealer showrooms.	9/29/66

First Generation

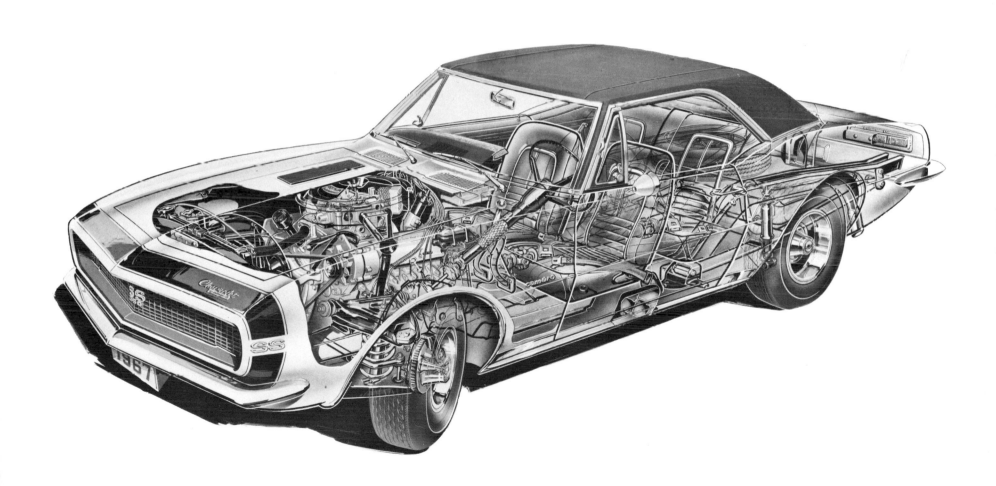

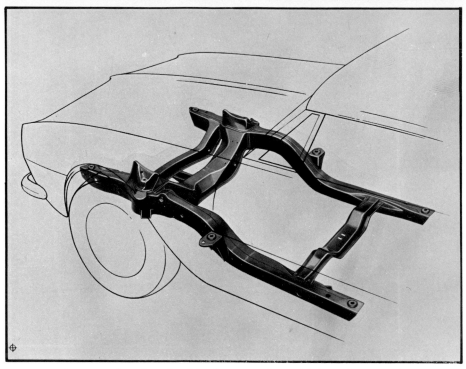

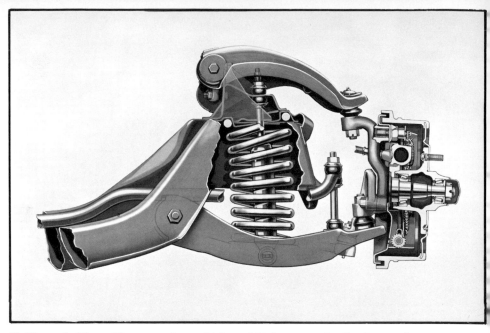

Camaros shared semi-unitized construction, with frameless main body section plus front subframe. Subframe carried engine, suspension, front sheetmetal.

Unlike early Chevy II's suspension, which used high-mounted coils, Camaro's A-arms were conventional. Subframe's rubber isolation prevented road harshness from entering passenger compartment. After 1967, Chevelle and Chevy II began to share Camaro's front suspension; later Camaros became pioneering testbeds for the handling improvements that filtered down to other GM cars.

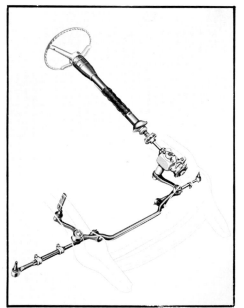

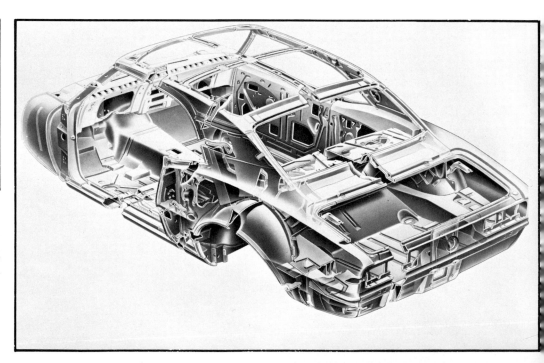

Early Camaro's steering linkage, unlike later version's, stood behind axles. Big rubber biscuits (above) isolated subframe bolts at four locations. Unit body (right) carried wash/dry rockers, flushed by air and water that entered at cowl.

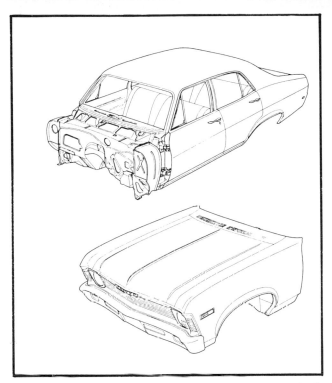

Many people believe Camaro was an outgrowth of the original Chevy II. Not so. Actually, the '68

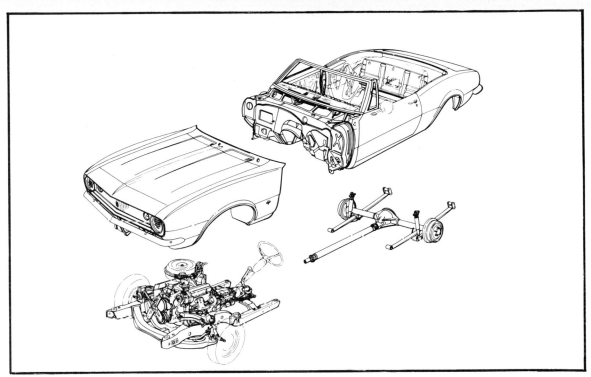

Chevy II grew from Camaro, which was all new for 1967. Both cars shared subframes, cowls, floorpans, brakes, and front axle/suspension. Single leaf rear springs, while similar, were shorter for the Camaro.

weight—was the lack of space in the rear floorpan and pickup area. Unitized rear construction gave more space for such components as the muffler, gas tank, and trunk.

Generally speaking, cars with entirely separate body-on-frame construction tend to ride more softly, more quietly, with less road rumble and greater smoothness than those with fully unitized bodies. Frame-integral (wholly unitized) cars like the early Chevy II and Falcon usually end up with noticeable road noise, body shake, and suspension reaction transmitted to the passenger compartment; an overall harshness of ride and feel that Chevrolet engineers considered unacceptable.

The classic 1936-37 Cord had a welded-on front subframe, but being welded, there was no isolation. Hudson, too, used a welded-on subframe for its 1948-54 stepdown models, its purpose being to make Hudson bodies more portable during the assembly process. And Chrysler Corp. cars of the early 1960's carried welded-on subframes. None of these, though, tried to isolate the subframe through rubber bushings.

It had been Mercedes and Opel who refined the bolt-on subframe during the 1960's with large, rubber-bushed attachments for isolation. The Opel Admiral in particular served as a developmental inspiration for Musser's R&D group and subsequent Camaro/Chevy II chassis engineering by Charles M. Rubly's staff at Chevrolet.

"Those cars that have really cleaned up the harshness factor," reflects Jim Musser, "are the ones with subframes, like Mercedes, which is really a unit-bodied car that puts subframes both front and rear, with a lot of isolation between the suspension and body."

Thus as the middle-ground option between pure unitized and full frame construction, Chevrolet engineers decided to go with a half-and-half arrangement—a liberally isolated front subframe and a unitized main body section. That basic theme hasn't changed in all the years Camaros have been made—both in the first generation of 1967-69 and the second generation of 1970½ to the present.

SEVERAL DIFFERENT TYPES of subframes and attachments were tried during the F-Car's initial development. According to Chevrolet chassis engineer Bill Lerg, "That project, which stemmed from the original X-Car [Chevy II], involved several concepts of the front subframe. These included wheelbarrow frames that went as far back as picking up the rear springs' front eyes. Those projects made us focus on what we could actually build—the assembly-line buildability of a frame-integral body versus a full chassis frame or something halfway in between.

"But we did try various other subframe configurations. I remember we initially wondered whether we could tie up higher on the cowl to get a triangulation effect to support the front end. That didn't have much practicality from a production standpoint. So it quickly evolved into a wheelbarrow-type subframe supporting the engine and front suspension, reinforced by the bolt-on front sheetmetal and tied into the unitized main body structure by four big bolts."

These bolts, as mentioned, were heavily bushed in rubber. The forward two attached under the cowl on each side, with the rearmost pair under the front seats. Several different types of rubber bushings were also tried—a research project spearheaded by chassis engineer Charles M. Rubly and carried out by Wes McCollum.

Bill Lerg continues: "There was a lot of thought that went into attaching the subframe to the main body section. The question was, 'How do we handle all the loading that's going to come in from various directions—the lateral, horizontal, and vertical loadings of driving and cornering plus the loads of engine, suspension reaction, and that sort of thing?' Quite a bit of work went into that.

"Charlie Rubly and his group actually were into various shapes on those big rubber biscuits—whether they should have sides to them, like a suspension bushing turned on end; or a cup shape or inverted cones or whatever."

After evaluating many bushing configurations, Rubly and his staff settled on a large double-biscuit mount that would absorb shock from any angle and yet be strong enough to outlast the vehicle and not erode nor compress with age and use.

AS IT TURNED OUT, both the F- and X-Car would share a good many major components: cowl structures, floorpans, the subframe and attachments, basic rear suspension systems, plus engines, transmissions, axles, brakes, and wheels.

The Camaro front suspension was designed afresh along very conventional lines and was soon shared with the 1967 A-bodied cars: Chevelle, Tempest, Special, and F-85 Cutlass. So were brakes, both disc and drum, and the rear axle. In fact, since the Camaro ended up using the same rear axle as the Chevelle, it took on a bit wider tread—front and rear—than originally specified, much to the delight of the body designers.

The Camaro's engine and transmission choices were shared with the Chevelle, too, and much of this commonality was passed along to the Chevy II for 1968. The idea, of course, was to give the 1967 Camaro as much interchangeability with other Chevrolet and GM nameplates as possible—to make sales volume high so all these cars' base prices could remain low.

CHEVROLET AND FISHER body engineers, including Jack Hakspacher, Don Urban, Douglas R. Remy, and Carl Jakust, worked out the structural details of the F-Car's main body section. It was (and still is) Fisher Body's responsibility to productionize and then to build and supply the body from the cowl rearward. Chevrolet tools and builds the front-end sheetmetal and chassis, but Fisher tools and builds the body from the cowl back.

The routine in developing any new Chevrolet product (except Corvettes) goes like this. Fisher, under the watchful eye of Chevrolet engineers and designers, takes the finished, full-sized clay styling mockup and works it up into a body that's buildable. Fisher's question becomes, Can these body panels be stamped out in high-volume production?

The body engineers make every effort to capture the designers' shapes, but they have to take into account the fact that sheetmetal will bend and stretch only so much. Hence there's always some compromise and negotiation between Design Staff and Fisher and Chevrolet body engineers.

Fisher plants and GM divisional assembly plants are always adjoining, so it's just a matter, as body engineer Don Urban puts it, ". . . of shoving the Fisher-built body through a hole in the wall," and placing it on the Chevrolet assembly line.

Before that, though, Fisher people have to engineer the structural elements of the body so it's buildable and hangs together. Things like door hinges, door inners, bracing around the cowl, reinforcements in the roof and at pillars—all these and hundreds of other unseen structural details emanate from Fisher Body Engineering. Approval, of course, has to come at every step of the way from Chevrolet body engineers.

The F-Car's floor structure, which was later shared with the Chevy II, became heavily reinforced to form a sturdy platform. The engineers integrated rear framing elements into the underbody to form good mounting structures for the Mono-Plate rear springs.

An interesting detail were the hollow rocker panels on either side of the floorpan. These were galvanized inside and out in Camaro coupes. In convertibles, the rockers used a heavier gauge sheetmetal plus an internal reinforcement. To prevent rust and corrosion inside the hollow rockers, Fisher Body engineers incorporated a forced-air system that ducted air from the cowl plenum chamber *through* the rockers, with an exhaust vent at the very rear. The idea—still used in today's Camaros—was to let air and rainwater flow through the rockers for a wash-and-dry effect. Water could enter to rinse out

dirt and salt, but the thought was to let the water be followed by a generous supply of air to dry out these totally inaccessible and very important stiffening structures. The 1963 Chevrolet and 1965 Corvair had similar rocker arrangements.

Door pillars, quarter panels, and the rear body plate for the Camaro were all conventionally welded to each other and to the underbody. So was the cowl itself, with its "saddlebag" ventilation plenum chambers. The housing board for the instruments became a welded, non-removable structural member into which the gauges, controls, and glovebox fit.

Chevy engineers specified a crossbow roof design, with the windshield header and roof siderails welded to the lower body through box-section front and rear pillars.

Altogether, the coupe body formed a very rigid unitized structure, yet ride harshness couldn't reach the passenger compartment because of the four big rubber biscuits up front (at the subframe) and the rear suspension's isolation via 10 more rubber bushings at all spring, shock-absorber, and shackle connections. No element of the Camaro's suspension had a metal-to-metal interface with the main body structure.

THE F-CAR'S REAR SUSPENSION used single-leaf (Mono-Plate) rear springs, as mentioned. This technology borrowed from GM's experience with the Chevy II and the Oldsmobile Toronado. Not that the Camaro's rear leaves were identical to the Chevy II's. They were 5.5 inches shorter, 2.5 pounds lighter, positioned differently, and came with different spring rates. Chevrolet later discovered wheel-hop and bottoming problems with the Camaro's single-leaf rear springs, but initially the decision looked like a good one, and for all but severe duty the Mono-Plate suspension worked out well.

Engineer Jim Musser comments, "The single-leaf spring is a fine concept, because the spring itself is shaped to have uniform stresses. It gives you a low-friction suspension—no rubbing between leaves. It does all the things it should do, but the windup resistance is less than with a multi-leaf spring. Incidentally, most of the development work on single-leaf springs was done by GM Engineering Staff, not by Chevrolet."

Adds his colleague, Chuck Hughes: "Single-leaf rear suspension works fine, and the only thing that a multi-leaf spring will do for you that a single-leaf won't is let you go to softer rates. You just can't store the same energy in that length of single-leaf spring. Another thing you run into with a single-leaf setup is what they call jitters, which means that at about 65 mph, the suspension becomes more sensitive than usual to tire out-of-roundness and imbalance."

Charlie Rubly's chassis group found that the Camaro's rear suspension gave less roll understeer when the rear springs were angled slightly inward at their forward ends. Normally rear springs lie parallel to a car's direction of travel, but computer analysis and actual experience showed the chassis people that this slightly splayed spring alignment gave better handling. Rear shocks, meanwhile, were mounted outboard of the springs and stood nearly straight up and down—an arrangement that wasn't ideal and that would change with the 1968 model.

GOOD HANDLING was one characteristic the engineering teams wanted to be sure to get into the new F-Car. In a paper prepared for the Society of Automotive Engineers' Detroit section meeting of Jan. 9-13, 1967, Chevrolet engineers Donald H. McPherson, Charles M. Rubly, and Victor D. Valade outlined the handling they were after in the Camaro and how they tried to go about getting it.

The computer was just coming of age in auto engineering, and the Camaro was one of the first American cars to make extensive use of computer aids. The engineers actually wanted to come as close as possible to *gran turismo* handling: sharply defined roadability, solid cornering, precise steering, good high-speed stability. Yet they also wanted comfortable riding qualities, with the road- and engine-noise isolation talked about earlier.

These were characteristics difficult to combine, particularly in a car that also had to become the engineering basis for a line of economical 2- and 4-door family sedans. Yet the Chevy engineers were determined to get them.

"These requirements led to design and development investigations of unusual scope

Engineer Don McPherson illustrates the role computers played in engineering Camaro's single-leaf rear springs. Computers were just coming of age during Camaro's development; the F-Car was among first to use them extensively.

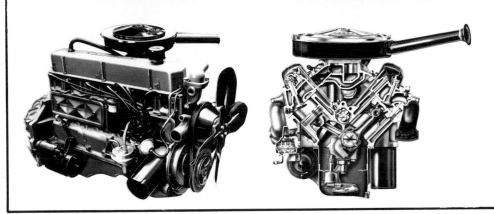

Chevy's 350 V-8 bowed in Camaro (right); 6 accounted for 25% of '67 sales.

Transparent quarter-scale body let engineers view stresses, parts relationships.

Open Camaros came with four "cocktail shakers," one at each corner. Each cannister contained a spring-loaded weight in a fluid, the purpose being to cancel out vibrations. The dampers added a total of 100 pounds to the car.

and magnitude," wrote the Chevrolet engineering team in its SAE paper. "One such investigation made use of modern computer techniques as an invaluable tool in analyzing and predicting complex interrelated vehicle characteristics."

Chevrolet assistant chief engineer Alex C. Mair noted further that, "It was probably the first time that we used the computer fairly extensively, because to get the handling of this car the way we wanted it, we didn't have enough time to do the old seat-of-the-pants work."

Computers would later be used even more when Chevrolet R&D became involved in the Camaro's 1967-70 racing career.

Chassis engineer Edward L. Nash adds, "I think we used more computer programing in that particular project than any car we'd done previously. We rather liked the handling of this automobile. The handling was computerized, if you will, and we had the cooperation of Don Nordeen over at GM Research at the time. He'd developed a computerized model of a vehicle for handling. We used this program in setting up the Camaro's spring rates, spring base front and rear, rollbar, roll couple control, and we were quite pleased, because it all appeared to be quite accurate."

As it turned out, the first Camaro handled even better than the computers had predicted it would.

CHEVROLET WORKED WITH the Engineering Mechanics department of GM Research Laboratories and first made out a definition and a set of target specifications of exactly the handling characteristics they hoped to incorporate in the production F-Car.

These were listed for both a one-passenger load and a 4-passenger load. Center-ofgravity locations were predicted at 49.3 inches behind the front wheels with a single-passenger load and 53.5 inches with four people aboard. Similar predictions were made for such variables as front and rear roll-center height, deflection steer due to aligning torque, roll rate, front roll camber coefficient, yaw inertia, roll inertia, and the front and rear roll steer range. Taking these parameters and feeding them into the computer, the engineers were able to analyze and fairly well predict how the "paper" F-Car would react and handle on the road.

Not only could they predict handling, they could crank in new factors at will—such things as different spring rates, rollbar stiffness, positioning of suspension members, tire sizes, and so forth. Each altered element would show up in the computer analysis with a new set of handling predictions. Thus the researchers didn't have to actually *build* dozens of different running prototypes to test these variables. They could shortcut the conventionl cut-and-try approach to handling and come up with figures, predictions, and eventually hardware that saved untold man hours.

"Through analog computer simulation techniques," wrote Don McPherson, "engineers from Research Laboratories and Chevrolet . . . predicted the directional control characteristics of this new car analytically, to an extent never possible by older traditional methods. In a relatively short time, as opposed to years by conventional means, the extreme speed and accuracy of the computer enabled these engineers to study the complex interrelationships of factors affecting vehicle handling behavior, over a wide range of conditions."

Since no one was yet sure what tire size the production Camaro would wear, initial programs used data for a conservatively small 6.50 x 13 tire. Anything that would handle with that petite a tire would do better with something bigger. Later, when the first cobbled Chevy II prototypes became available for testing, the engineers ran handling trials using both 6.50 x 13 tires and 6.95 x 14's.

F-CAR PROTOTYPES consisted of first-generation Chevy II's reworked with an early version of the new subframe and front suspension. These "component cars" or "mules" were outfitted to look and handle as much as possible like what engineers felt the Camaro would eventually be.

The mules were handbuilt, of course. One had the in-line Chevy 6, and two others carried V-8's. Cobbled, lowered, rearranged body types included the convertible as well as the coupe with seating set rearward on the 108.1-inch wheelbase to approximate the loading conditions of the Camaro-to-be.

Those early prototype vehicles were first driven only at GM's Proving Grounds near Milford, Mich. Among the initial tests were those to measure directional control response. The engineers were amazed at how well these cars handled right out of the box. Usually the first component cars need a lot of refinement.

"One pleasant aspect of the early program was the surprise we received when we first drove our prototype," recalls body engineer Jack Hakspacher. "It was so pleasant, so quick, so responsive that we knew we had something extra. We were kind of surprised because our competition was, in our opinion, a little bit on the harsh side, and when we finally had our prototype put together and drove it, we were really surprised and pleased."

Chuck Hughes, who was attached to the Proving Grounds at the time, adds, "It was immediately apparent to all of us that it was one helluva car when we picked up the first prototypes. I remember it was such a glorious day when prototypes were actually driveable. When we drove them out from Detroit to the Proving Grounds, it was really a beautiful time for us . . . ."

Alex Mair concurs. "I went on a couple of the development trips, and the notable thing is that we, for the first time, felt quite good about the handling we'd developed. The car **was** very responsive."

A PERIOD OF STATIC TESTING and drive testing followed. Static tests consisted not only of torture-twisting prototype metal bodies but also of building miniature clear-plastic scale models of Camaro bodies and subjecting them to bending, vibration, and stress tests.

This is common practice at GM. The clear-plastic model is usually ⅓ to ½ scale, accurate in every detail. The thickness of the plastic is also scaled precisely. Then by subjecting the model to torsional and beam bending tests, stresses in the plastic can be pinpointed and measured in terms of heat buildup and molecular distortion. Stress areas can even be photographed on heat-sensitive film. Results of these tests with the plastic models can be scaled up to equal the same conclusions in metal. It's a clever shortcut to see how well the body engineers did their job.

On-the-road tests in component cars and prototypes included a number of long runs around the nation—from Detroit east into New England, south as far as Florida, and west to California and the GM Desert Proving Grounds outside Phoenix.

"In addition to long runs . . . we used to take shorter one-day trips across the state and back," reports Carl Jakust. "When we went on those, we'd drive not just the Camaros but also the comparison cars—Mustangs, Barracudas, Firebirds, and others. We'd drive over courses that we'd picked out so they gave us handling roads and some super-highway travel and other conditions."

Chuck Hughes amplifies: "On those one-day trips, every 20 miles we'd change cars, and we might even do a loop of particular roads to see how each car behaved. We could compare cars that way.

"We also took longer trips in the prototypes, of course. In February or March, 1965, we went down to Florida, as I recall. Camaro trips were always fun. It was a pleasure to go down to Florida with them, or to California, and to swing through the twisty mountain roads . . . .

"So many times when you're out on a test trip, you drive through some town in Kansas or someplace like that, and no one takes any particular notice that you're in a brand-new car. Even in New York City, people rarely notice. But we drove these cars out to Los Angeles—this was back with the first Camaro before it came out—and we drove down Sunset Strip with this yellow-and-red Camaro, and we were absolutely *mobbed!* People followed us all over town.

"I remember it was kind of gratifying that California people picked it up so readily. It was a fun time. We stopped and let people look at the car. This was in June, 1966, months before we introduced the car . . . ."

THE CAMARO'S single-leaf rear suspension did cause a few early problems, as already mentioned. One was wheel hop, especially under hard acceleration.

Chassis engineer Charlie Rubly later explained to a reporter that wheel hop hadn't become apparent until the larger V-8's—the 350 and 396—were teamed with 4-speed gearboxes. And a different type of wheel hop showed up under some rare braking conditions, particularly during simultaneous braking and cornering.

After several months of prototype testing, the brake-hop problem cropped up when one of the engineers happened to be downshifting and hit the brakes at the same time on a washboard road. The car went into a violent hop-skip situation. Other cars, including the Mustang, would do the same thing under those conditions, but the single-leaf rear springs, being soft, accented the problem.

For 1968, staggered rear shocks corrected wheel hop to a large extent, but they hadn't been incorporated into 1967 production. Instead, a track bar became standard with all 1967 V-8's more powerful than the base 210-bhp 327. Actually there were two different types of track bars used in '67—one single bar on early models (on the passenger's side only) and later a set of five bars or links that connected the axle and Mono-Plate springs to the rear undercarriage.

Chassis engineer Ed Nash feels the judder and wheel-hop problems weren't entirely the fault of the Mono-Plate rear springs. "I can't say that the single-leaf springs were the cause of all tendencies for wheel hop. That's pretty basic, I think, to any sort of Hotchkiss drive mechanism. Staggered shocks were evaluated in all four corners of the rear axle. We picked the combination that proved the most efficient."

The idea of trying staggered rear shocks came initially at the suggestion of staff engineer Paul King, who later became chief engineer of Chevrolet pasenger cars. King had been watching movies of the axle-hop phenomenon. He noted that the 1966

After F-Car's general body shape crystalized, engineer Charles Rubly (above in vest) and stylist John Schinella took clay model to LTV windtunnel near Dallas to test Camaro's aerodynamics. Wet ink droplets on model's surface showed air currents that led to changes in front fenders, bumper pan. Links on disc beneath model attach to sensors that register drag, yaw, directional stability, etc. Spoilers were added to Z-28's as a result of windtunnel data.

Chevrolet engineers (l-r) Bonvallet, Rider, Hughes, and Harlow prepare for a cross-country shakedown in winter 1965. Component cars or "mules" were built to duplicate Camaros as closely as possible, but masking hid identity. One convertible and two coupes made trip, which tuned handling and body.

Linked by CB radio, drivers could talk and compare notes en route. While much testing took place at GM's Michigan & Arizona proving grounds, on-the-road miles turned up problems not evident elsewhere.

Later prototype, looking more like real thing, made countless routine laps around Milford oval.

Toronado had used them successfully, but the situation was slightly different because the Toro didn't have a live rear axle. Later, when the staggered shocks proved their value on the 1968 Camaro, King applied for a patent on them but found that Packard already held patents dating from 1936.

Jim Musser, who at that time was assistant chief engineer of the Chevrolet product design group, also worked on staggered shocks. "Later it became apparent to us *why* they worked," reminisces Musser. "When you get into a hop condition, you're winding up and unwinding the springs very quickly. It's a high-frequency thing that feeds itself and tends to pivot around the shock absorbers. You're winding up and bending the springs, but the shocks don't see too much movement.

"Remounting both shocks either fore or aft of the axle doesn't do much good, because all you do is change the nodal point where the springs bend. But if you stagger the shocks, axle windup does work the shocks, and they break up the symmetry of the reaction, so the windup on both sides isn't the same. It really turned out to be a very effective, simple solution to a complicated condition."

ON THE PROBLEM of rear-end bottoming under load, Robert L. Dorn, who served as Camaro/Nova chief engineer 1969-72 but who also helped develop the first Camaro, feels, "Bottoming stemmed from a number of things that happened early in the development program. The car was originally styled too high off the ground and with too-small tires. The small tires had been a cost consideration. Then, when we got the Camaro out on the road, it didn't look good; it stood too high up in the air.

"At the same time they started to lower it, they put on bigger tires—went to a 70 series—and then you didn't have enough ride travel in the rear anymore. What you did was to ride around on the jounce bumpers if you put any sort of load in the rear seat or trunk. We revamped the 1968 models so they'd have more rear suspension travel."

As an aside, for owners of 1967 Camaros who still have problems with rear-end bottoming, air shocks are the answer. These can be inflated to raise the car an inch or so at the rear, which makes the change in riding height hardly noticeable but gives enough suspension travel to prevent bottoming.

Early prototype testing of the F-Car showed that the convertible body had a tendency to shake under certain conditions. "The body didn't have full enclosures to give it additional strength," says Jack Hakspacher, "and in our opinion, since our development people were pretty fussy and didn't like the convertible's response over rough roads, we put on these big cylindrical harmonic dampers."

Alex Mair recalls that, "The bodywork was well set by the time I got to Chevrolet, with the exception of the Camaro convertible. We had to do a great deal of work on the convertible because, since it was semi-integral, we found a fair amount of torsional shake. We actually had to hide harmonic dampers in each corner of the car. We called them *cocktail shakers*.

"These were tuned dampers—sealed steel barrels with spring-loaded weights riding in hydraulic fluid. The purpose was to have the weight oppose torsional vibrating frequencies. They were heavy, about 25 pounds each, and we wouldn't get away with anything that heavy today because of weight restrictions. Corvair convertibles used similar cocktail shakers from 1965 through 1969, as had the big unit-bodied Thunderbird and Lincoln convertibles of the late 1950's and early '60's.

"The cocktail shakers made these Camaro convertibles quite free from shake, yet they still had the softness a convertible always has. You know, convertibles are really free from impact, but the trouble is that they shake. Charlie Rubly did a lot of that work, even though he was actually in the chassis end of the business."

Chevrolet engineers still note that pre-production prototypes amazed them by their lack of road harshness, excellent ride, silence, and solid handling qualities.

Chapter Three
Designers at Work

WE STEP BACKWARD in time now to pick up the Camaro's styling evolution—the point at which the car began to take shape. Word had come down in early Aug. 1964 that there *would* be a Chevrolet sporty car for 1967 to challenge the Mustang directly. General Motors now realized that the 1965 Corvair couldn't match the Mustang's engine and option versatility.

The news pleased Chevy general manager Bunkie Knudsen mightily, and GM's Design Staff, as mentioned, had been hoping for just such an opportunity and wasn't caught at all unprepared.

The man with overall charge of the F-Car's styling was GM design vice president William L. Mitchell. Mr. Mitchell, now retired, also oversaw the second-generation Camaro's styling—the 1970½'s—and he makes no bones about which version he likes best. "The 1970½ Camaro," he says, "is a designer's design; but that first series was designed by committee."

What Mitchell means is that certain specifications for the 1967 Camaro were laid down early by Chevrolet engineers and management to accommodate the practicality of the 1968 Chevy II. While the Camaro came first and did get the major styling and

engineering emphasis, everyone realized that the Camaro had to be the specialty car and the Chevy II had to be the volume seller. Thus the new 1968 Chevy II could and did dictate certain terms and conditions to the Camaro design team.

Two of the compromised dimensions that left the Camaro's designers less than ecstatic were: 1) the tallness of the cowl, and 2) the short dash-to-front-axle span. Comments David M. Holls, then Chevrolet group chief designer, "We were a little unhappy with those dimensions, but they were just requirements—a tooling requirement and a cost consideration."

THE CAMARO'S CHIEF DESIGNER for both the first and second generation was Henry C. Haga. Haga reported to Dave Holls, who in turn reported to Chevrolet/Pontiac executive designers Charles M. (Chuck) Jordan and Irvin W. (Irv) Rybicki. All, of course, had a good deal to do with the Camaro's eventual shape, but most of the actual drawingboard work and clay modeling came out of Henry Haga's Chevrolet Studio Two.

As it happened, that particular studio also had responsibility for the design of the

Chevrolet designers and engineers took Mustang as their point of departure and determined to beat it in every way—in dimensions, styling, performance.

Henry Haga's studio evolved "high-bone" fender line for first-generation Camaro, sketched here in the extreme.

By Dec. 1964, designers had settled on "Panther's" full-width loop grille and *its basic body configuration.* *Rear began with tail lamps similar to Firebird's.*

rebodied 1968 Corvette. Haga had helped productionize the 1965 Corvair, and he'd been instrumental in styling the Super Nova showcar. So all three—Corvette, Corvair, and Super Nova—influenced the Camaro's design.

Henry Haga was working as design director for Opel in Germany when we contacted him for his remembrances of the F-Car's early styling development. Haga wrote back a long, very informative letter detailing his involvement with not only the first-generation Camaro but also the second. He headed the design teams that created both cars. Here are parts of Haga's letter:

"To start with, the men in Chevrolet Studio Two—the designers, modelers, and engineers—were all auto enthusiasts. We were pretty excited when we found out we had a chance to design an all-new, 4-place sporty car that would eventually compete with the Ford Mustang."

The General Motors design theme of that era was termed *fluid,* and it emphasized a look based on an interesting proposition. The GM theory held that if you take a heavy wire frame and bend it into the basic 3-dimensional outline of the car you want, then stretch thin canvas over the frame, and if you finally blow compressed air gently up into

the bottom of the canvas envelope, you get a very natural, free-flowing, unartificial body shape. This fluid form showed up most strikingly in the 1965 crop of General Motors cars, and it continued as a corporate look for a number of years thereafter.

"The canvas-stretched-over-wire theme," continues Henry Haga, "served to give the Camaro its own character and separated it from the Mustang approach, which was much stiffer and more angular."

The 1964 Super Nova showcar set the first direction for the Camaro-to-be, although it was used only loosely as a model. The Corvette and Corvair also entered into the Camaro's early styling, as Haga explains further.

"The continuity of the GM design concept was consistent even though the 1965 Corvair design started in an advanced studio, headed by Ron Hill, before it became a production studio project in the Chevrolet studio. I was privileged to be production studio chief in charge of the Corvair at that time. Later, when we started to design the 1967 Camaro, we again chose the fluid theme as being the most proper direction for us to pursue.

"We felt very strongly about reducing design to its simplest form, using only one

And in Feb. 1965, refinements brought Camaro to its final "face." Haga's studio was also working on '68 Corvette, so rear aspect showed resemblance.

peak down each body side, interrupted by accented wheel arches. The profile of the car also was very simple, using the classic approach of crowned fender lines, with their high points directly above the accented wheel arches.

"We purposefully avoided any contrived design lines and superflous detail. Even the execution of the wide, horizontal-loop front end and grille, with its hidden headlamps in the Rally Sport variant, was as pure in content as we could make it."

Haga goes on: "The F-Car design had one major flaw, though, and that was *proportion*. The cowl was too high, and the front-wheel location stood too far back; what we call the 'dash-to-axle' ended up too short. Those were areas and dimensions shared with the Chevy II for 1968. Also, the execution of the side rear-quarter window didn't help the car's sportiness, because it made it look more like a conventional hardtop than an exotic sports car."

ON THE BRIGHTER SIDE, a last-minute decision to use the Chevelle rear axle gave the F-Car a wider tread than intially planned. This came as a pleasant surprise for the designers, because the wider tread meant a huskier, more potent looking car.

Another fortuitous result of having to use the Chevelle axle was that the 1968 Chevy II also benefited. "The rocker and wheel tread," notes Dave Holls, "is much wider than it would normally have been for a sedan of that type, and that came as a result of the Camaro's influence. The Nova's dash-to-axle also grew larger than it would have been otherwise."

The F-Car, which was code-named XP-836 and *Panther* by the designers, took shape very rapidly, going from drawings to clay to fiberglass within a few short weeks. Two styling nuances were the curved side windows and the Coke-bottle-shaped sideview, enhanced with bright rocker trim on the RS models and given a slimming up by using black paint beneath the lower door line. The use of black here blended with the road shadow to give the Camaro's body a slimmer, less bulky look—an idea borrowed from the Corvette and Super Sport versions of the Chevelle.

A styling headache stemmed from an early engineering specification to use 13-inch wheels and tires. "Because of an improper definition of what the car was going to be, there was some confusion about wheel and tire sizes," continues Hank Haga. "I remember at one point that we had a tremendous amount of open wheel cut surrounding the tires. Because of the Camaro's marketing philosophy, we had to make the car offer a full range of tire sizes. This left the poor car with the smallest tires at a great disadvantage."

Another frustration came from the 2-body-type limit imposed by Chevrolet management: coupe and convertible only. "We weren't able to include a fastback in the Camaro line," laments Dave Holls, although one was mocked up in clay as a response to the Mustang fastback.

Other body styles considered for the first-generation Camaro were a 2-place convertible and a 2-door station wagon, or Kammback. These were based as much as possible on existing sheetmetal tooling, which by then was pretty far along. But both the 2-place ragtop and the wagon turned out to be mere styling exercises, because there wasn't a budget to put them into production.

Budget restrictions, in fact, were quite drastic in this car, because it had to compete with the Mustang, and one of the Mustang's main selling points was price. Price consciousness became less of a problem after about 1973, when the competing standard-sized ponycars dropped by the wayside.

THE F-CAR'S INSTRUMENT PANEL borrowed heavily from the 1968 Corvette-to-be. The man who headed the Camaro interior design team was George Angersbach, who had responsibility for all Chevrolet sporty and small car interiors, including Corvair and Chevy II. Angersbach reported to Chevrolet chief interior designer Donald Schwarz.

"We were working on the 1968 Corvette at the time we were doing the Camaro interior,"notes George Angersbach. "The '68 Corvette was originally slated to come out as a 1967 model. But then there was some uncertainty about the timing. We wanted to

"Oil-cooler" hood louvers for SS were originally intended to be functional, but water leaked in. Early RS grille beamed lights directly through grids.

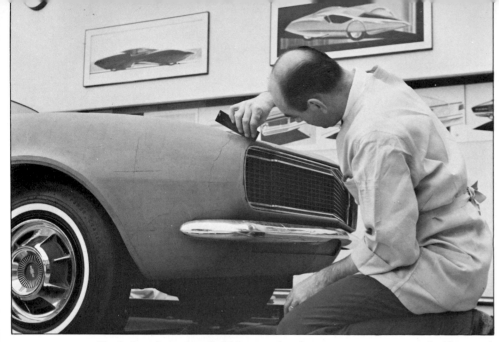

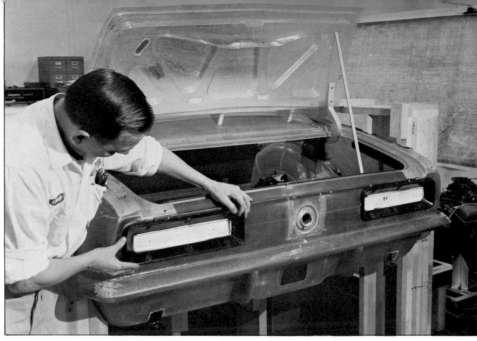

Final clay above gets finishing touches for management approval. Afterward, technicians built fiberglass mockup with all panels detailed to inner surface

shapes. Note transparent decklid. When sheetmetal came back from presses, panels were hand-assembled to check fit and that hinges mounted properly.

Camaro shared theme of large twin dials with 1968 Corvette, but central panel and console took their shape from Super Nova. While a male stylist is shown sketching console gauge cluster, it was actually designed by a woman, Sue Vanderbilt. Firebirds used same basic panel design from 1967 through '69.

Around Mar. 1966, Firebird and Camaro designers experimented with 2-passenger version of F-Car. Different grilles and lamps were grafted to same clay.

be sure we didn't lose that 1968 Vette instrument panel theme—the two big dials—so we put them into the Camaro, too.

"Actually, those two cars—the Corvette and the Camaro— we tried to keep them a family, where you'd have the out-and-out sports car and then you had the sporty 4-place coupe and convertible to go along with it. We put some of the Corvette flavor into the interior on purpose."

Donald Schwarz broadens the Camaro's interior development by adding, "The Super Nova was the first car we did of that type. The basic philosophy of the Super Nova's interior was what ended up in the first F-Car—the two large dials. But the control area of the Super Nova started at the top of the instrument panel, then sloped *back* toward the seats and blended with the tunnel console to form a divider down the middle of the car. The console flowed back between the rear seats. It was a lot like the 1963 Riviera.

"When they decided to go ahead with the F-Car, we had to get practical. We couldn't do the tunnel all in one swoop, because Camaros with bench seats wouldn't have consoles. So we ended up doing the design with the center panel rolled under instead of outward."

On the interior door trim, the designers decided they wanted a one-piece, molded, contemporary look and settled on a new and fairly expensive material for the Custom interior door panels—a foam-filled laminate. Cadillac had used the same material previously, as had the Corvette. The idea was to give a softer feel to the Custom panels, plus good insulation, and yet have some bulkiness and plushness to puff out around emblems and brightwork.

"We modeled this foam-filled panel in clay," says Don Schwarz, "and I clearly remember that it meant going to a great deal of expense for tooling and production. We had a meeting in the Design Center auditorium. Mr. Knudsen was general manager at the time, and the Fisher Body people didn't really want to do these molded door panels for what amounted to a low-budget car.

"Mr. Gathman, who was head of Fisher Body, was invited over to the meeting by Mr. Knudsen, and Knudsen said, 'This is what we want,' and Gathman said, 'Fine, that's what we'll do,' and they did it. The design came out fairly close to what we intended."

WITH NO SPACE FOR extra gauges within the F-Car's twin dials, and with the air-conditioning outlet taking up the top portion of the 1967 Camaro's central control panel, a question soon arose: Where to put the additional gauges that performance enthusiasts were bound to want?

The answer came from another interior designer, Sue Vanderbilt. Sue suggested and executed not only the design of the 3-dial console gauge cluster for the '67 model but also the 4-gauge "sawtooth" console pack for 1968-69. Ms. Vanderbilt later became one of the chief designers of Chevrolet interiors. The mounting of these gauge clusters on the front of the tunnel console came as a compromise after no more comfortable spot could be found.

The 1968 Firebird, by the way, placed all working gauges into the big right-hand dial and used the same basic instrument panel for 1967-69 as the 1967-68 Camaros. Pontiac had gotten permission to join the F-Car program in Feb. 1966 and quickly designed their own grille, front-end sheetmetal, rear trunk panel, and the hashmarks on the rear fender flanks. Pontiac also made some mechanical changes, including multi-leaf rear springs from the beginning plus the use of their own engines, transmissions, wheels, bigger tires, etc. The Firebird story, though, deserves a separate book, and it's one we hope to publish soon.

IN THE F-CAR'S FINAL DESIGN stages, Chevrolet sent a quarter-scale model of the coupe to the Ling-Temco-Vought aircraft windtunnel near Dallas. This took place in Feb. 1965, during one of Detroit's worst snowstorms. A staff stylist, a clay modeler, and a Chevrolet engineer were glad to get out of the cold and accompanied the model to the relatively balmy climes of Texas.

"This was at a time when we were first getting into aerodynamics," comments engineer Victor Valade. "We wanted to make sure the car had some good aerodynamics. This was still early enough in the first Camaro program so minor changes could be made in the body shape."

The windtunnel tests spanned 11 days, and a few small changes were made as a result to clean up the Camaro's airflow characteristics. One involved reworking the front valance panel beneath the bumper. Another had to do with reshaping the front fenders slightly. Both were carried through into production Camaros.

The quarter-sized model still had the original narrow tread called for in early Camaro specifications. It was trimmed to duplicate a full-sized car carrying two people and V-8 engine. Airflow was recorded by using wet ink spots on the surface of the model and also by a force balance under the tunnel floor.

Special instrumentation measured lift, drag, side force, body roll, pitch, and yawing moment. The results let Chevrolet check on ventilation, power consumption, traction at high speeds, and crosswind sensitivity.

A positive-pressure area showed up at the base of the windshield, as expected, so that's where the cowl vent and cold-air pickup for the aircleaner went. Chevrolet had been using cold-air induction on race cars since 1963, when Paul Prior, working in Vince Piggins' area, improved Daytona lap speeds of 1963 Impalas by 2-3 mph. Ducted air cleaners were thus offered and homologated with the first Z-28 introduced at Riverside in Nov. 1966.

And because of negative air pressure near the very rear of the coupe, the Z-28 got a spoiler. In fact, engineer/author Paul van Valkenburgh, working in Chevrolet R&D at the time, used the windtunnel figures to design not only the Z-28's rear spoiler but its front air dam as well. And designer/engineer Larry Shinoda of Chevrolet's special projects studio used this same windtunnel data to design the Z-28's cold-air hood scoop—the 1969 option with the rear-facing opening. More about that, though in Chapter Six.

Designers converted Camaro to 2-seater by removing eight inches behind door. Station-wagon version of 1967 Camaro was also built during same period.

Chevrolet stylists regretted not getting permission to do a Camaro fastback to compete with Mustang 2 + 2, but despite little hope they mocked one up anyway.

Chapter Four

The Camaro's Debut

WHILE ALL THIS DEVELOPMENTAL activity was going on inside General Motors, the motoring press and the public became increasingly anxious to see Chevrolet's answer to the Mustang. Word leaked out that such a car *was* in the works, and in 1965-66, a few sightings were made of disguised prototypes.

One of the first speculative articles about the F-Car appeared in POPULAR SCIENCE for Dec. 1965. Auto editor Jan P. Norbye made some amazingly accurate predictions about the car. He correctly gave wheelbase, engine and transmission choices, and general proportions of the Camaro.

Norbye assumed, as did many GM insiders at the time, that the F-Car would be called *Panther*. He also predicted that it would be based on the first-generation Chevy II, with its fully unitized body and Falcon-like high front-coil suspension.

As more rumors leaked out, the Camaro came to be called not only Panther by reporters and magazine writers but also F-Car, Chevette, and XP-836. Articles appeared in many of the major car magazines, and MECHANIX ILLUSTRATED ran a fairly inaccurate cover story, with equally inaccurate drawings, in its June 1966 issue. This was two months after the *New York Herald Tribune* and other papers had run spy photos of test vehicles on the road. These spy shots were accurate in nearly every detail.

ON JULY 1, 1965, Elliott M. (Pete) Estes came over from Pontiac to Chevrolet and replaced Bunkie Knudsen as general manager. Thus it was under Estes that the Camaro would be finished, named, launched, and marketed.

Interestingly, Estes happened to live right across the street from Ford Div. general manager Donald N. Frey. Whether Estes and Frey ever compared notes on the Camaro and Mustang isn't recorded, but their living so near one another gave rise to a story (apocryphal) that's still told today.

GM engineers, so the story goes, talked about having Estes drive home all manner of odd cars that the corporation owned at that time. Frey, of course, would be peeking out from behind discreetly parted curtains as Estes arrived home each evening, and Frey would be left to speculate which of these oddballs and assortment of cobbled prototypes, etc., might be the real "Panther."

Three months before the new car hit dealers' showrooms, Estes announced to a gathering of reporters that it would be called *Camaro*.

"Why Camaro?" asked *Detroit News* business writer John Gill at the press conference.

"That's one of the general manager's prerogatives—the naming of a new car,"

Chevrolet used cutaway cars plus movies, stage revues, and ads to introduce '67 Camaros.

replied Estes, and then he quipped, "I went into a closet, shut the door, and came out with the name."

One behind-the-scenes story about naming the Camaro illustrates the agonies Chevrolet management had to be going through at the time. According to engineer Doug Remy:

"The advertising agency called for nameplates on the front fenders and, of course, you can't really build and sell a car without a name. Unfortunately, the final selection of an exact name became delayed.

"In Engineering, we'd gotten well beyond our normal release date for nameplates . . . . We were making drawings of nameplates of any name that seemed likely to be a winner. We released *Panther* first, and dies for that nameplate were actually completed. Other names were also released for tooling—there were three in all, although the only other one I remember for sure was *Commander.*

"When we finally got word that *Camaro* would be the approved name, we were down to only 6-8 weeks before deadline. By that time, only an all-out, maximum overtime effort would get the nameplates for S.O.P. We probably blew some $100,000 in unused tooling, but it was worth it because Pete Estes surely picked a winner!"

CHEVROLET LET IT BE KNOWN that the word *Camaro* had a meaning. It was a French word, so the publicists said, that meant "comrade, pal, buddy, friend." Linguists soon took issue, though, saying that *their* French dictionaries carried no such definition. A few noted wryly that if anything, the word *camaro* refers to a type of shrimp in Spanish.

TIME Magazine published an account of the controversy, prompting Chevrolet to issue a press release with a photocopy of an old French dictionary page that did, indeed, list the "comrade, pal, buddy" definition.

A teaser ad campaign preceded the Camaro's introduction. Chevrolet had gone through a slow year in 1966, with sales lagging 9.7% behind record 1965. Corvair sales had taken a drastic slide since the Ralph Nader episode, and Chevy sales manager Robert D. Lund calculated that pre-selling the Camaro, even at the expense of the Corvair, couldn't hurt overall business.

The Camaro entered dealer showrooms on Sept. 21, 1966 and drew considerable attention. To help launch the new car, Chevrolet commissioned the Jam Handy organization of Detroit to put together not only a half-hour movie about the Camaro but also a fairly elaborate stage revue.

The color movie, called simply *The Camaro,* was narrated by cartoonist Milton Caniff and gave a brief developmental history of the F-Car, with interesting glimpses into styling, engineering, and testing activities. Dave Holls, Don McPherson, Alex Mair, and Bob Lund made cameo appearances. The movie was shown extensively in local theaters and on television.

The stage revue, called *Off Broadway,* included four different road companies, each performing identical material but each assigned to a different area of the country. Together and within a very short time, these four troupes introduced the 1967 Camaro in 25 U.S. and Canadian cities.

Each of the four companies had its own small orchestra, a line of dancers, a chorus of singers, and a 1967 coupe and convertible onstage. AUTOMOTIVE NEWS called the *Off Broadway* revue, ". . . some of the fanciest, gaudiest, and costliest entertainment ever to hit the boards."

Still another early Camaro promotion consisted of a new line of women's fashions. These were created by designer David Crystal of New York. Known as the *Camaro Collection,* the half-dozen dresses were "named for Chevrolet's sporty new personal-sized car. The introduction of the fashions for motoring reflects the prominent role of the automobile in the modern woman's world." Dresses in the Camaro Collection cost between $20 and $40 and were available in 450 shops across the country.

(Right) *Linda Hock models dress from Camaro Collection at '67 Chicago show.*

First-Generation Camaros

Amply equipped 1967 convertible displays SS plus RS packages, bumper guards, luggage rack, and Rally wheels that denote front disc brakes.

Motor Trend's John Ethridge takes pre-production SS-350 for a spin (note optional headrests) during July 1966 press preview at GM proving grounds.

IF YOU BOUGHT a new Camaro for 1967, you'll remember having to study a long list of factory options and dealer-installed accessories.

Marketers call it the "building-block" concept of selling, and since the Mustang had honed this approach to a fine edge, the Camaro took it a step further by offering an absolutely staggering variety of 81 factory options plus 41 dealer accessories. The choices and combinations were virtually endless and certainly confusing, especially since options could be combined in many different ways as, for example, the Rally Sport with the Super Sport package.

Prices began at $2466 f.o.b. Norwood, Ohio—the only GM plant then assembling Camaros—for the base 6-cylinder coupe. The lowest priced, stripped convertible cost $2704; add another $26 for the larger 6 (RPO L-22) or $106 for the base V-8 (the 210-bhp 327).

At that point, though, you started to look at the Rally Sport package, various more potent V-8's, and the bumblebee-striped Super Sport option. Designer Dave Holls, by the way, mentions that the bumblebee idea came from the C-Type Jaguar and that since everyone else was putting longitudinal stripes on car hoods and decks, ". . . we decided to do something different."

The Super Sport package came initially only with the 350-cid V-8, an engine exclusive to and introduced with the 1967 Camaro. In later years, of course, the 350 became one of Chevrolet's most popular engines and a Camaro standard, but for 1967 no other Chevy offered it.

On Nov. 22, 1966, the L-35 396-cid V-8 was announced for the Camaro in its 325-bhp

form, and on that same date Turbo Hydra-Matic became available in Camaros for the first time, but only with the 396. The 350 and 396 V-8's demanded buying the SS package (RPO Z-27; $210.65), which included heavy-duty suspension, the bumblebee hood stripe, D70-14 Firestone Wide Oval redwall tires on 6-inch rims, raised hood with finned "oil cooler" inserts, underhood insulation, and Super Sport identification emblems on the gas cap, steering hub, and front fenders. The SS-396, by the way, came to $395 or nearly $200 more than the SS-350. In Mar. 1967, Chevrolet announced that the bumblebee stripe could be ordered separately—without the SS package—on any Camaro, but again only in black and white as before.

Later in the model year, the 396 would become available as RPO L-78 in the 375-bhp version. And on Dec. 11, 1966, the legendary Z-28 package, with its 302-cid V-8, made its debut. The Z-28's main purpose was to qualify and quantify the Camaro for SCCA Trans-Am sedan racing. For the full Z-28 story and its doings on the track, see Chapters Six and Seven.

THE WEALTH OF RPO choices left many a Camaro buyer boggled and still remains a source of confusion for restorers and collectors. Let's see, though, whether we can't make some sense out of the RPO list.

The 1967 Camaro offered two basic interior trim levels—base and Custom. Carpeting and bucket seats were standard in both, with a front bench seat (Strato-back, RPO AL-4; $26.35) also available in both versions.

The base interior had flat embossed door panels with bolt-on armrests, exposed door

Custom '67 interior came with molded door panels, seat color accents. Of interest here are the power windows, air conditioning, and gauge cluster on console.

Base '67 interior shows plainer seat, door panel with applied armrest.

Console gauge pack automatically included tach in right-hand dash pod. Optional Strato-back bench (right) boasts armrest, puts shift selector on column.

handles, and single-color seats in four all-vinyl fabrics: black, blue, red, or gold. The base bench front seat was not available in red.

The Custom interior (RPO Z-87; $94.80) came with a different embossed seat and door-panel pattern; contrasting color accent bands on the seats; one-piece, foam-filled door panels with recessed handles in a built-in armrest. Seven colors graced the Custom interior (black, gold, turquoise, red, bright blue, parchment, and yellow), with accent bands in parchment (for seats in gold, black, or bright blue); black bands with red or parchment seats; dark turquoise on turquoise; and dark gold on yellow. The Custom front bench could be ordered only in black, bright blue, or gold.

The Strato-back front bench, by the way, had individual, hinged backrests and a wide, folding central armrest. Another interesting seat option was a fold-down rear seat (RPO A-67; $31.60), available for both the coupe and convertible. This had a carpeted back and laid down for additional cargo capacity. The idea came from the Corvair.

Additional items in the Custom interior group included underhood insulation, molded trunk mat, deluxe steering wheel, rear-seat armrests with ashtrays, and round courtesy lights in the coupe.

Worth noting, too, was a secondary, so-called Special Interior group, which included chromed plastic windshield pillar moldings, bright-trimmed pedal pads, and chromed inside roof-rail moldings.

Column-mounted shifters came as standard equipment in all Camaros, with floor selectors or shifters available only when you ordered: a) the tunnel console, b) a 4-speed or heavy-duty 3-speed manual transmission, or c) Turbo Hydra-Matic.

The tunnel console (RPO D-55; $47.70), made basically of styrene plastic but with

cast-metal storage compartment door and ashtray cover, had a light in the rear that came on when either car door opened.

A special 3-dial gauge cluster (U-17) that cost $79 could be ordered in V-8 Camaros only for placement at the leading edge of the console. With this gauge pack, the right-hand dashboard dial housed a 7000-rpm tach, while the three console gauges registered (left to right) fuel, engine temperature, clock, oil, and amperes.

ON THE EXTERIOR, one step above the standard Camaro meant the Style Trim group (Z-21; $30 on the convertible, $40 on coupes), which consisted of twinline body pinstriping, anodized aluminum wheel-lip moldings, and the bright roof-gutter moldings.

Then came the Rally Sport package, RPO Z-22, costing $105.35 extra in 1967 and available for either the coupe or convertible. The RS included a special full-width grille with electrically operated headlight doors; parking lamps in the front valence panel (the standard grille incorporated exposed headlights and grille-mounted parkers); full red tail lamps with the backup lights again in the valence panel; RS emblems on the gas cap, steering hub, front fenders, and grille; twinline body pinstriping; wide anodized-aluminum rocker moldings with black-painted rocker bottoms; bright wheel-lip accent moldings; plus chrome drip moldings for the coupe.

By way of contrast, the standard tail lamps used the same bezels as the RS, but half of each lamp was given over to the backup lamps; also the standard steering wheel didn't have chrome metal spoke covers and used a plainer horn button.

The Rally Sport package could be ordered, as mentioned, with the Super Sport group

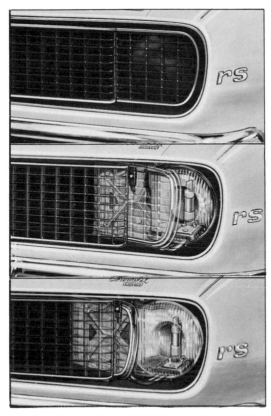

Hidden headlights in 1967-69 Rally Sport grilles opened, shut automatically with normal switch. Twin electric motors powered headlight doors.

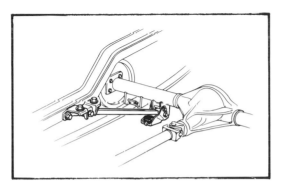

1967 Camaro V-8's with horsepower greater than the base 327 got a traction bar on passenger's side to counter wheel hop with single-leaf rear springs.

Several big Chevy dealers offered custom 427 installations in '67 Camaros. Among the better known, Dana Chevrolet in Los Angeles converted about 35 cars under direction of race driver/mechanic Dick Guldstrand and owner Peyton Cramer. Conversions were usually expensive, but Dana Camaros ran like stink.

From 1967 through '70, Camaros were assembled (left) in Norwood, Ohio and Van Nuys, Calif. About 25% came with front discs (center); none had much trunk space—8.3 cubic feet in the coupe and 5.6 in the convertible (right). Super Sport's bumblebee stripe on nose (below) was inspired by C-Type Jag.

or in any other Camaro RPO combination except those that conflicted directly, like the Style Trim package.

For wheel dress-up, three optional styles of wheelcovers could be ordered separately with all packages. The simulated wire wheelcovers (PO-2; $73.75) were popular for the RS, while the deep-dish "tulip" covers (PO-1; $21.10) were often ordered with the SS. There was also a mag-style wheelcover, N-96, for $73.75. The 5-slot Rally wheels (RPO P-12) were often specified with disc brakes and/or the SS and Z-28.

Other noteworthy RPO's included the following:

Item	RPO	Price	Item	RPO	Price
Deluxe steering wheel	N-40	$7.00	Rear window defroster	C-50	21.10
Walnut-grain steering wheel	N-34	32.00	AM pushbutton radio	U-63	57.00
Tilt steering column	N-33	42.15	AM/FM pushbutton radio	U-69	133.80
Headrests, pair	AS-2	52.70	Stereo tape system (req. radio)	U-57	128.10
Front shoulder belts	AS-1	23.00	Rear speaker	U-80	14.00
Front shoulder belts, deluxe	A-85	26.00	Remote outside mirror	D-33	9.00
Tinted windshield	A-02	21.00	Electric clock	U-35	15.80
Tinted glass, all windows	A-01	30.55	Cruise Master speed control	K-30	50.05

The vinyl roof cover (RPO C-08; $73.75) came in black or fawn only. The convertible top was available in black, white, or medium blue. Standard was a hand-operated convertible top, with a power top (RPO C-06) listed at $52.70 extra.

Four-Seasons air conditioning (RPO C-60) listed for $356 extra and included a

Chevrolet RPO Classifications

Notes: RPO stands for **Regular Production Option** and designates an option that comes from the factory rather than one that's dealer installed.

Generally speaking, Chevrolet RPO's with prefixes A-D are for body items. F-J designate chassis, and K-L are engine options. Several letters are omitted from the RPO alphabet, notably E, I, O, R, S, T, and W.

Sometimes several RPO's come as a package, with no additional charge for the included pieces. For example, RPO U-14 is a special instrument package that includes RPO U-35, an electric clock, at no extra charge.

At other times, one RPO demands the addition of others. Example: In 1967-69, you couldn't order RPO Z-28, a high-performance engine and trim package, without also ordering a mandatory 4-speed transmission and front disc brakes, both costing extra.

RPO Prefix	Equipment	Examples
A	Seats & windows	AL-4 Stratoback seats A-02 tinted windshield AU-3 power door locks
B	Mats & guards	B-93 door-edge guards B-37 floormats
C	Roof & vent system	C-08 vinyl roof cover C-60 Four-Seasons a/c C-50 rear window defogger
D	Add-on body items	D-80 rear spoiler D-35 dual outside mirrors D-55 floor console
F	Suspension	F-41 special, front & rear
G & H	Axles	G-80 Positraction G-92 high-altitude ratio H-01 3.08:1 ratio
J	Brakes	JL-8 four-wheel discs J-65 sintered metallic linings
K	Engine accessories	K-24 PCV equipment K-30 cruise control

RPO Prefix	Equipment	Examples
L	Engines	LT-1 360-bhp 350 V-8
M	Transmissions	M-21 close-ratio 4-speed
N	Steering, exhaust, some wheels	N-33 Comfortilt wheel N-10 dual exhaust system
P & Q	Wheels & tires	P-01 full wheelcovers PL-4 white-letter F70-14
U	Electrical	U-69 AM/FM radio U-14 special instrumentation UA-1 heavy-duty battery
V	Radiator & bumpers	V-01 heavy-duty radiator VF-3 deluxe bumpers
Y & Z	Special packages and miscellaneous	Z-28 high-performance 302 Z-22 Rally Sport (early) Z-85 Type LT

(Above) *Chevrolet's ad agency, Campbell-Ewald, set up this shot in summer 1966, even before Camaro got its name. Red fiberglass proto lacks nameplates, rolls on 13-inch tires. Trailer-mounted "billboard" stood blank* *when photo was made. Artist later stripped in yellow SS coupe.* (Right) *Production 1968 Camaro negotiates San Francisco's twisty Lombard Street, boasts Style Trim Z-21 group: bright belt, rocker, and wheel-lip moldings.*

61-amp alternator, heavy-duty radiator, and viscous-drive fan. Power steering was recommended with this option. And power side windows (RPO A-31)—a very rare accessory in early Camaros—cost $100.10 additional.

ON THE MECHANICAL SIDE, the '67 Camaro's standard non-power steering was set up with a 24:1 ratio or four turns lock to lock—pretty slow for a sporty GT car. The standard ratio for convertibles or air-conditioned cars was even slower: 28:1.

But there was a bright side, because regular power steering (RPO N-40; $84.30) boasted a 3-turn, 17.5:1 ratio. And for an additional $15.80 you could order the short-spindle-arm N-44 quick-ratio steering, which brought manual down to an 18:1 ratio and made power 15.6:1.

Standard brakes on Camaro coupes were the 9.5-inch drums all around, shared with the Chevelle, Chevy II, and Corvair. The Camaro convertible, however, being slightly heavier, came with 11-inch drums up front. All drum brakes used 2.5-inch front shoes and 2.0-inchers at the rear. Sintered metallic linings were optional (RPO J-65; $37.90). And for $79, you could get the optional 11-inch ventilated front discs (RPO J-52), which came with or without vacuum assist (J-50; $42.15). Or you could buy the vacuum booster for any brake setup separately.

One of your best buys for the dollar was the heavy-duty suspension package, which cost only $10.55 and carried RPO numbers F-21 and F-41. This included higher-rate springs and stiffer shocks and came standard with the Super Sport and the 275-bhp 327.

Standard tires came in size 7.35 x 14 on 5-inch wheels, and 13-inchers were never offered. The D70-14 Wide Oval redwall SS tires and 6-inch wheels could be ordered for any Camaro, and there was also a heavy-duty 7.35 x 14 whitewall available.

(Above) Ray Brock takes Chevrolet's Walt Mackenzie for a tour of Ontario speedway in white & blue, 396-engined convertible that paced 1967 Indy 500.

Camaro Waikiki became a 1967 styling exercise and showcar. It used Di Noc woodgrain, rattan seat inserts, wire wheels, square headlamps, modified grille.

Positraction cost $42.15 (G-80), and for an additional $2 you could specify the axle ratio of your choice—this with any rear end, not just Positraction.

TURNING NOW TO THE ENGINE compartment, General Motors at that time had an unwritten rule that no car could produce more than one horsepower per 10 pounds of vehicle weight. That "law," while broken more than once, was generally adhered to, at least nominally.

Since the Camaro's weight averaged out at around 3250 pounds, the most potent factory engine allowable was the 325-bhp 396. Chevrolet at first hadn't wanted to offer even that much power in the Camaro, but the Mustang's 390 V-8 out-horsed the Camaro 350 by 25 bhp, and Chevy wasn't about to be beat in any way by the Mustang. So the 396 became a defensive response after a month of so of Camaro production. And it fit under the Camaro hood with amazing ease.

The 396-cid V-8, also called the "semi-hemi" or "porcupine" V-8, was a small-bore version of the original Mark II 427 "mystery engine" introduced at Daytona Beach in Feb. 1963. The Mark II, later known as the Mark IV, were V-8's of a completely new design, having no relation to the 1958-65 W series that had been made in 348-, 409-, and 427-cid sizes but never as a 396.

The "porcupine" name, though, went back to the W series, which used flat-faced combustion chambers and the block deck shaved at 29-degree angle from the horizontal (most V-8's are 45 degrees). This gave the W's combustion chambers an elliptical shape at the top, so that by staggering the valves across the head they could be made larger in diameter. This poked the valve stems up at all different angles and locations atop each head, giving the engine its porcupine nickname. Only with individual ball-stud-mounted

In Aug. 1966, designers began work on 1968 Camaros, suggested this early revision. Ideas that didn't make it include chromed rockers, low-profile grille.

Another factory showster, this one for 1968, was called Caribe and carried a small pickup box behind roll bar. Thin windshield pillars without a header, custom wheels, and reflective tire sidewalls stood out among Caribe's nuances.

Stylists changed 1968 Camaro's Custom interior in several ways: pad now wrapped around dash ends; seats, console, and wheel were different. Stirrup

selector for automatic trans became a safety factor, and lack of ventipanes put air outlets into panel. Woodgrain highlighted Style Trim or Custom interiors.

Tachometer surrounds clock in 1968 Camaro Tick-Tock-Tach, which came with console gauge pack. Instruments had silver instead of black backgrounds.

rockers could such a system work, but work it did, and it was carried over in modified form to the 396.

The Mark IV in a 396-cid version was first available in the 1965 Corvette, and it also became available in the Chevelle as the SS-396 in mid-1965. Late in Jan. 1967, the Camaro's 325-bhp 396 was joined by a 375-bhp version for installation by dealers. And for 1968, two more 396's were offered—a 350-horse in-betweener and a heavy-duty, aluminum-head edition of the 375-bhp V-8. The three 350- and 375-bhp 396's were intended mostly for drag racing.

But we're getting ahead. The engine/drivetrain charts on pages 138-142 list all available factory engines for all years of Camaros, so we'll hit only the high points here.

The 350, as mentioned, was new to Chevrolet for 1967 and became a Camaro exclusive that year. It was created by taking the 327 and increasing its stroke from 3.25 to 3.48 inches. Very little else had to be changed, and as most Chevrolet buffs realize, the so-called *small-block* family of V-8's ranges from the 265 of 1955 through the 400-cid engine introduced in 1970. Constant improvements were made in such areas as gasketry and casting techniques, but all Chevrolet V-8 engines in sizes 265, 283, 302, 305, 307, 327, 350, and 400 remained basically the same.

The big-block Chevy, meanwhile, included V-8's with displacements of 396, 402, 427, 454, and (for racing) 510 cid.

Nor was the 327 any slouch, because for years it reigned as the Chevrolet standard bearer. In the 1964-65 Corvette, the 327 in fuel-injected form put out 375 bhp. Some 22 327's were cast in aluminum for racing, but none made it into Camaros.

And at the economy end of the Camaro's horsepower scale were two 6's, basically identical and respectable performers in their own right. Road tests of the day put the 155-bhp 6's fuel economy at 19.1 mpg overall—not bad for a sporty car with a top speed of 107 mph. The 350 V-8's top speed, by the way, was listed by enthusiast magazines at around 120 mph.

On a totally different level and gone into in more detail in our *Camaro Racing*

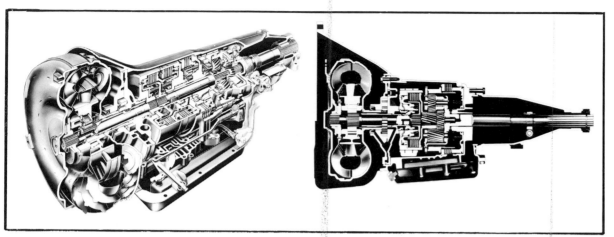

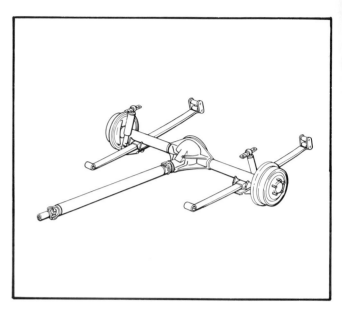

Turbo Hydra-Matic (left) became available for all engines in 1968, including the 6's. Torque-Drive semi-automatic (right), offered in 1968-69 only, cost $65, amounted to Powerglide minus self-shifting abilities.

1968 CAMARO CHASSIS

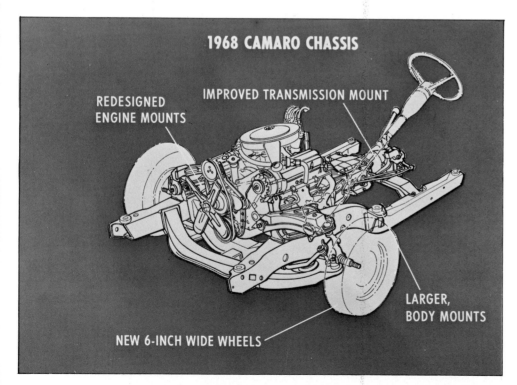

REDESIGNED ENGINE MOUNTS

IMPROVED TRANSMISSION MOUNT

LARGER, BODY MOUNTS

NEW 6-INCH WIDE WHEELS

NEW STAGGER MOUNTED SHOCK ABSORBERS

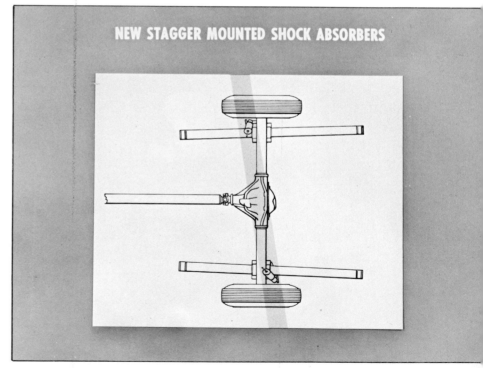

Besides subframe revisions shown, Camaro V-8's for 1968 got wider main and rod bearings. Standard wheels went to 14x6 instead of 5-inchers used before.

Staggered rear shocks became a big '68 improvement: one shock ahead of the axle, one behind. They countered wheel hop, eliminated need for traction bar.

Chevrolet's 396 in its 325-bhp form proved the Camaro's most popular big block, and the same powerplant was available in 350- and 375-bhp versions.

Finned 1967 "oil-cooler" hood ornamentation carried over for 1968 SS-350, but the SS-396's received new set of 8-blip inserts with chromed wire mesh.

Coupe displays Style Trim group (Z-21), with bright moldings above and beneath windows, on wheel lips, rockers. RS had backup lamps in bumper pan.

Nickey Chevrolet in Chicago and Bill Thomas of Anaheim collaborated on 427 conversions. Included were F-41 suspension, power disc brakes, Muncie 4-speed, special tires, and dressup, all for $4060.

chapter: In Oct. 1967, two Smokey Yunick-prepared coupes— a Z-28 and an SS-396—set 115 class records at Bonneville. The Z-28 topped 174 mph and the 396 did better than 183 on the salt.

INDIANAPOLIS MOTOR SPEEDWAY officials chose the Camaro as 1967's Indy 500 pace car. Because of a rainstorm, the race had to be stopped and restarted, so the 1967 Camaro paced that year's event twice. In 1969, a Camaro was again tapped to pace the Indianapolis classic.

The 1967 pace car was an RS/SS-396 convertible with Turbo Hydra-Matic, driven by triple Indy winner Mauri Rose, who also happened to work for Chevrolet engineering at the time. Approximately 100 1967 Camaro pace-car replicas were built, most of them SS-350's with Powerglide. Indy dignitaries and the motoring press used these cars around the speedway for about a week. Later, the pace-car replicas were all sold to the public as used cars.

The year 1967 turned out to be a good one for Chevrolet—second only to record-breaking 1965 in total sales. One factor was the Camaro, which now more than compensated for the faltering Corvair. Early demand was so high for the Camaro that dealers sold 46,758 before 1966 was out. In all, 220,009 Camaros found owners in model-year 1967 (see page 137 for complete production figures).

Chevrolet general manager E.M. Estes estimated that if a month-long strike in the winter of 1967 hadn't stopped production at the Norwood plant, dealers might have sold an additional 16,000 Camaros that year. By and large, though, all ponycars enjoyed excellent health in 1967, taking a full 13% of the domestic market. The Camaro

Italian coachbuilder Frua displayed rebodied 1968 Camaro hatchback at Paris show. Special wheelcovers went on car right after these photos were taken.

was joined by the Cougar and Firebird as new ponycar nameplates for 1967, and the Barracuda got a new body style in convertible, coupe, and fastback configurations.

Chevrolet owner surveys showed that Camaro buyers tended to be young, educated, and affluent. Median age was 31, one notch above the Corvette. Over 60% had gone to college, and median income was $10,400 (or about $20,800 in 1979 dollars). Approximately 25% of Camaro buyers were women, mostly single. Half of all Camaros were purchased by people who hadn't owned a Chevrolet before, and 33% had "seriously considered" the Mustang before buying a Camaro.

The 1968 Camaros

To the untrained eye, the 1968 Camaro looked like nothing happened. But a lot did: dozens of major and minor changes on and beneath the surface took place between the 1967 and 1968 models.

The easiest way to tell a '68 from a '67 Camaro is by the little square sidemarker lights on each fender. Sidemarkers were mandated by federal law for all 1968 U.S. cars.

Another giveaway is the lack of ventipanes on the 1968 Camaros. The '68's standard grille came to more of a prow, too, with rectangular instead of round parking lamps and a silver-painted mesh instead of black.

The 1968 tail lamps had vertical splits down each bezel, with the Rally Sport using four red lenses and non-RS cars incorporating the white backup lens in the same pod. These pods, incidentally, interchange with the '67's but aren't the same.

The RS, SS, and Style Trim groups went into 1968 pretty much intact, although the RS no longer had pinstriping. Pinstriping had to be ordered separately (RPO D-96; $13.70) and ran along the body side ridges instead of near the fender peaks. Some photos show this pinstripe extended up over the trunk rear panel.

New RS emblems were entirely different, and instead of 1967's wide, bright aluminum rocker trim, each 1968 rocker carried a thin molding in the Coke bottle groove and then used black paint beneath that to blend with the ground shadow (except on dark-colored RS cars).

The SS-396 boasted a black trunk rear panel with all but black paint jobs, and the

Houndstooth seats became available for 1968. Door panels now wrapped up onto sills, with Custom panel (above) again carrying molded armrest plus carpeted lower section. Base panel (below) had applied armrest but hidden pull.

Illustrations point out differences in Custom (above) and base (right) interiors for '68. Custom seats came in more colors, but their accent stripes were gone.

Dull-finish black trunk end panels graced all 1968 Super Sport 396's except those with black paint jobs.

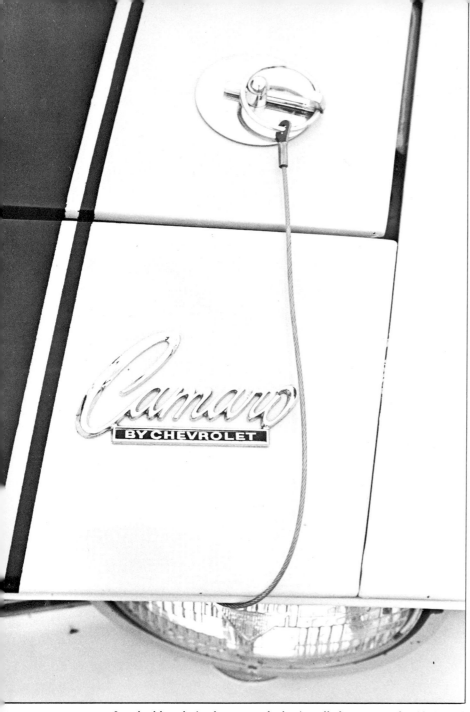

Leashed hood pins became a dealer-installed accessory for 1968, and emblems now made the name Camaro *prominent instead of the word* Chevrolet. *Previous emblems reversed size of* Chevrolet *and* Camaro.

Multicolored rainbow bumblebee stripe became part of trim package called "Customized Camaro," introduced as a mid-year promotion to highlight Hugger Month.

46   THE GREAT CAMARO

SS-396 also received a special hood with 8-blip simulated air intakes. The SS-350 hood for 1968 kept the '67's fluted "oil cooler" inserts. And an interesting addition to the SS package for '68: finned front brake drums as standard equipment.

Front discs were still optional, and late in the 1968 model year 4-wheel disc brakes became a service option for the racing Z-28 only. It would be 1969 before 4-wheel discs would be listed as an RPO, and even then only about 200 sets were sold. Chrome dressup appeared on SS-350 and SS-396 valve covers, aircleaners, and oil fillers. The 375-bhp SS-396, by the way, cost $500.30 or about $100 more than the basic Z-28 package.

The SS's bumblebee stripe came in three versions for 1968. One wrapped around the nose as before, and a second type appeared later in the year—a stripe that formed a moustache midway down the nose and then swept rearward along the ridge of each door. The third type was a multi-tone, ribboned bumblebee introduced in mid-year on the so-called "Customized Camaro" offered as a sales package during "Hugger Month."

The multi-tone bumblebee stripe had narrow bands of bright colors. These alternated from light to dark and finally blended with the body color. The "Customized Camaro"sales package included this stripe along with four new colors: LeMans blue, Rallye green, Brite green, and Corvette bronze. The package likewise included houndstooth upholstery, mag-spoke wheelcovers, whitewalls, and a rear-deck spoiler.

Vinyl roofs (RPO C-08) were available in black and white only, and body paint stripes came in only those two colors, too. The standard convertible-top color was white, but black and blue could be ordered with any exterior hue.

Rally wheels with different center caps than in 1967 were optional in 14-inch (RPO ZJ-7) or 15-inch (P-28) sizes, but only if you also opted for front disc brakes. The ZJ-7 Rally wheels cost only $31.60 a set—a bargain in anybody's book.

The F-41 heavy-duty suspension still listed for $10.55, but for 1968 the more powerful V-8's started getting multi-leaf rear springs. These carried five leaves, with different

There seems to be some question whether 1968 Rally Sport fender scoop really made production (above, below). RS had black paint below rocker moldings.

rates suited to individual engines. They came standard with all 350 and 396 V-8's; also with the 275-bhp 327 when ordered with a 4-speed. According to Chevrolet engineer Bob Dorn, the 1968 Camaro got considerably more rear suspension travel and thus became a more liveable car.

TURNING NOW to the 1968's interior, the big news inside was Astro Ventilation, heralded by little signs on each ventless front window. This flow-through system used ball nozzles at either end of the instrument panel which, when teamed with the regular kick-panel vents, cooled driver and passenger top to bottom. You could drive with all windows rolled up, because air entered through the cowl and exhausted via hidden vents in the door jambs.

Camaro interiors again came in standard and optional Custom trim levels. The '68 models had new door panels that wrapped up onto the window sills, but the standard panels were plainer, as were the standard bucket seats. Expanded vinyl made the seats "breathe" better for 1968. An interesting addition to the 1968 interior was a woven seat

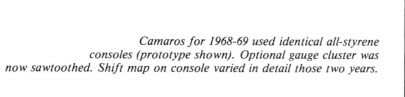

Camaros for 1968-69 used identical all-styrene consoles (prototype shown). Optional gauge cluster was now sawtoothed. Shift map on console varied in detail those two years.

Early styling proposals for 1969 Camaro began in Feb. 1967 with grille-less look, similar to Pininfarina's Telaio Corvair showcar. Side windows also began to take on B-pillar treatment that led to 1970½'s roof. Mercedes 300-SL inspired wheel brows, according to Henry Haga.

By May 1967, the 1969 Camaro's styling came into focus, but with a wider grille grid, larger parking lamps, and different fender louvers. Around back, designers tried to get the lamps to appear wide, thus segmenting lenses in thirds.

Camaro studio turned out special Camaro for French ski champion Jean Claude Killy, with roof rack, built-in spoiler. Killy made Chevy ads at the time.

Beginning on Feb. 14, 1969, Camaro got a new base V-8. This 307-cid engine replaced the 210-bhp 327, and the high-performance 327 gave way to L-65 350.

insert in black-and-white houndstooth. But the all-vinyl 1968 Custom upholstery patterns didn't include contrasting accent framing as in 1967.

The '68's main gauge cluster stayed the same as in '67, but the big twin dials now showed silvery faces instead of black ones, plus shallower lens cones. Padded windshield pillars complemented a new Custom instrument panel pad that draped down in a wide, inverted U near the doors.

Custom (Z-87) and Special (Z-23) interiors (the Z-23 was an out-take of the Z-87) included woodgraining on the dashboard central control panel. A grab handle above the glove compartment came with the Custom group, and the word *Camaro* appeared on the glovebox door.

The 1968 console (D-55; $50.60) wasn't anything like its previous self. All plastic, it perched atop the tunnel and had little walls at each side to keep things from sliding off. The console gauge cluster (U-17; $94.80) was different, too: four rectangular faces in a sawtooth pattern. When you ordered these console gauges, you also got the Tick-Tock-Tach, a 7000-rpm tachometer with an electric clock in its center. This went into the right-hand dial of the big twin gauges. The Z-28's tach went to 8000 rpm.

ALL 1968 ENGINES remained essentially the same as in 1967, although the small-block V-8 got larger-diameter main bearings for the new season. Aluminum cylinder heads for the L-89 396 V-8 were listed as an option on an option, and this 375-bhp engine also had a specific 4-barrel Holley carburetor and other high-performance goodies.

A noteworthy and rarely seen 1968 Camaro transmission option was the Torque-Drive semi-automatic, introduced on Feb. 24, 1968 and available only for the 6. Torque-Drive cost $68.65, and what it amounted to was Powerglide minus its ability to self-shift.

Gone were the automatic valve body, governor, vacuum modulator, and high-speed

O.J. Simpson poses with his 1969 SS-396 convertible.

Base '69 convertible makes interesting comparison with Style Trim-equipped coupe. As before, Style Trim was out-take of RS—minus hidden headlights,

backup lamps under bumper, RS emblems, white parking lenses, bright moldings around windshield. Both options included pinstriping and wheel accents.

downshift. Gone, too, was the clutch pedal. Torque-Drive made the driver the transmission's brain and muscle. He merely selected low or high range (or reverse) by hand as needed, using the positively notched column selector. Volkswagen offered a similar semi-automatic for about $65 more that Chevrolet's.

Standard and heavy-duty 3-speed gearboxes for the 327 V-8 (L-30) had identical ratios, but gears inside the H-D unit were stronger. The normal 3-speed used a column shifter while the H-D had a floor lever.

CAR LIFE Magazine voted the 1968 Camaro Z-28 one of the 10 best cars of that year, and NASCAR handed all '68 Camaros its Industrial Award of Excellence. Camaro sales continued to climb, bettering the 1967 tally by about 15,000 cars. One factor in the Camaro's growing market strength was its great success in Trans-Am sedan racing, where it took the championship in 1968 by beating a lot of Mustangs. Mustang sales, in fact, were sliding a lot faster than Camaro sales were growing.

The 1969 Camaros

A lot happened to the Camaro in 1969. It was still basically the same car as in 1967-68, but it looked considerably different and had quite a few changes in powertrains and options.

For example, 4-wheel disc brakes became optional for *all* Camaros in '69, not just the Z-28. Variable-ratio power steering was another new option, as were body-colored Endura soft front bumpers and cold-air ram induction for the SS and Z-28. Camaros became available in 2-tone paint combinations for the first time, and the selection of vinyl roof colors went from two to five.

Chevrolet discontinued the 327 V-8 in Feb. 1969 and a new 307-cid engine replaced it as the Camaro's standard V-8. The L-65 350 superseded 1968's high-performance 327, giving the 1969 Camaro two 350's and four 396's in addition to the Z-28 302, the base 307, and the two 6's.

According to designer Henry Haga, whose Chevrolet studio had charge of styling both the first- and second-generation Camaros, the 1969 model's wheel-lip brows were

derived from the Mercedes 300-SL gullwing. The 300-SL, you'll recall, had very pronounced brows above each wheel cutout. In the 1969 Camaro, these brows were toned down, stretched out, and debossed as speed streaks that blended into the body side metal.

The standard 1969 Camaro grille became deeper set and bolder. Tail lamps were longer and thinner, segmented in three angled sections, with backup lamps integral in standard form. Pressed-in hashmarks appeared just ahead of the rear-wheel cutouts, and the Coke-bottle rocker indent disappeared in 1969.

Fourteen new exterior colors, with six 2-tone combinations, made their debut, and four more hues carried over from 1968. Exterior striping came in red, black, and white. There were four fancy stripe configurations: 1) wheel brow accents (RPO D-96), standard in the Rally Sport but not available in the Super Sport group and optional in combination with the Z-28 and DX-1; 2) front fender sport striping (D-90), included in the SS package—a swash up the leading edge of each front fender, diminishing along the fender peak and door; 3) a modified bumblebee (DX-1) that swept back up the center of the hood; not offered with the Z-28, SS, nor D-90; and 4) the Z-28's longitudinal racing stripes atop the hood and decklid.

THE EVER-POPULAR Rally Sport package for 1969 again included hidden headlamps, but the headlight covers had glass ribs in them so if the doors accidentally stayed shut, oncoming drivers could still see the lit lamp behind it at night. Another standard feature of the 1969 RS was headlamp washers—twin nozzles that squirted water onto the lenses on command. These washers were optional on other Camaros.

The RS also took on non-segmented tail lamps, with the backup lights again in the valence panel. Other RS items included bright accents on the rear fender louvers, bright wheel-lip moldings, black-painted rockers on lighter colored cars, and RS emblems all around. The RS option this year (RPO Z-22) had gone up to $132, but you could still combine it with the Super Sport group.

An out-take of the RS was the Style Trim option. This included just the bright

Sport striping RPO D-90 became part of SS group. The SS-396 coupe above includes optional ZJ-7 Rally wheels, ZL-2 cold-air hood, body-color Endura bumper. The SS-350 below sports hubcaps and trim rings. For 1969, the 8-blip hood became standard on all SS models, phasing out finned "oil-cooler" type.

Spoiler D-80 could be ordered for any Camaro, not just Z-28. Engine dressup kit, shown above on 300-bhp L-48 350, was also available for all V-8's in 1969. Variable-ratio power steering speeded up parking, gave driver more road feel.

Liquid tire chain (RPO V-75; $23.20) helped low-speed traction on snow and ice, mounted inside trunk, had remote release. Other Chevys offered it, too.

moldings of the RS plus the fender paint stripes and bright headlamp bezel moldings.

The Super Sport package (RPO Z-27; $312) was highlighted by a black-painted end panel on the trunk and the same 8-blip hood as in 1968. But this time these two items came with all SS engines, not just the 396. Engine dressup, the D-90 paint striping, bright rear-fender louver moldings, and the usual SS emblems inside and out were additional parts of the 1969 Super Sport option.

Inside the '69 Camaro, you could choose between the standard interior, the Custom interior (Z-87), and the Special interior (Z-23), the latter being a short version of Z-87.

Don Schwarz's studio completely re-did the 1969 instrument panel for '69, with square gauges instead of the round ones of 1967-68. This square-faced panel was shared with the 1969 Chevy II, but the pads were different. A 2-spoke steering wheel became standard, with front headrests likewise and the Strato-back bench seat option discontinued.

Standard door panels were modified slightly for 1969, and the bucket embossing ran horizontal instead of vertical. The Custom door panels, meanwhile, carried over from 1968 with minor changes, as did the optional tunnel console, because its shift-pattern plate was different. The 1969 Custom buckets had a bit less wrap, and their embossing this time ran vertical instead of horizontal.

As part of the Custom interior group, you got bright pedal trim, a glovebox light, woodgraining on the instrument panel and steering wheel, heavier body insulation, a trunk mat, grab handles on the dash panel and doors, and a choice of solid vinyl colors (black, blue, medium green, dark green, red, plus black/white houndstooth framed in black or ivory vinyl. Later in the 1969 model year, houndstooth yellow and houndstooth orange were added.)

In mid-year, a "Pacesetter Value Package" coincided with the Camaro's being chosen as the 1969 Indy 500 pace car. This package included the 350 V-8, power front disc brakes, whitewalls, and wheelcovers. The package cost $147 less than it would have if the parts were bought individually in 1968.

Astro ventilation continued, with its nametag now above the left air outlet on the dash. Air outlets were square for 1969, higher up, and adjustable in four directions.

Air conditioning (C-50; $376) was available for all '69 Camaros except Z-28's and the 375-bhp 396's. The special instrumentation package (U-17) continued unchanged, but with the Tick-Tock-Tach square this year instead of round as in 1968.

A 10-inch-wide rearview mirror replaced the 8-incher used previously, and a woodgrain 3-spoke steering wheel was optional. The anti-theft steering column locked the wheel and, with a column-mounted shifter, the shift lever, too. The new ignition lock stood on a different type of energy-absorbing column. Instead of a mesh sleeve, the '69 version used a deforming ball-and-sleeve arrangement.

I F YOU ORDERED power steering for your 1969 Camaro, the only type offered was variable-ratio. This meant an overall 15.5:1 ratio on center and 11.8:1 toward the locks. Total wheel turns were reduced to a quick 2.16, but driving straight down the road the car had good wheel feel and wasn't touchy. When parking or turning sharply, the steering ratio accelerated so that the front tries crimped faster.

You could order an even faster variable power-steering ratio as RPO N-44. This came automatically when you got power steering in the Z-28 or SS. The N-44 option was required for all 350- and 396-engined Camaros, and it meant only 2.06 turns of the wheel lock to lock, with ratios of 14.3:1 and 10.8:1 overall.

Non-assisted steering likewise had an N-44 fast-ratio option that reduced wheel turns from the normal 4.8 to 3.5 (21.6:1 ratio instead of 24.0:1). And an extra-fast manual ratio for the Z-28 came in at 17.9:1 or 2.9 turns of the wheel.

Rear suspension was again single-leaf for 1969 Camaros with 6-cylinder engines and the base V-8's. Five-leaf rear springs came standard with all higher horsepower V-8's and, according to Chevrolet's literature, ". . . all rear leaves are selected from a family of springs by Electronic Data Processing, which indentifies the correct spring for the weight of the vehicle by including the optional equipment ordered by the customer."

RPO F-40 designated a heavy-duty optional front and rear suspension system; F-41

Camaros paced Indy 500 in 1969 as well as '67. Harlan
Fengler (inset) piloted the '69 pacer, while triple Indy winner Mauri Rose
drove the 1967 car. Rose also served as a Chevrolet engineering
consultant at that time. Both pace cars had 396 engines with Turbo
Hydra-Matic, and both were easily up to the required 120-mph track speed.

was a performance suspension package that included not just heftier springs but also larger anti-roll bar and shocks; and G-31 noted a special rear spring only.

The JL-8 4-wheel disc brake option was, as mentioned, offered for all 1969 Camaros, not just the Z-28. Priced at $500.30, it didn't find too many takers. Positraction and 15-inch Sport wheels were required with the 4-wheel discs, and E70-15 nylon 4-ply tires came as part of the package.

These 4-wheel discs, by the way, had the 11.75-inch rotors and 4-piston fixed calipers adapted from the Corvette. All mounting hardware, a new axle housing, etc., were specific to the Camaro, though, and didn't interchange with the Vette.

The regular 2-wheel front disc option (J-52) was revamped for 1969 and carried a floating single-piston design instead of the 4-piston fixed caliper used for 1968. Front-wheel discs were required with all 1969 350 and 396 V-8's. And vacuum assist (J-50) was mandatory with these disc-brake systems.

Standard brakes for the smaller engined Camaros improved by using the finned front drums from the 1968 SS package.

The year 1969 marked the first time Turbo Hydra-Matic could be ordered with any Camaro engine. You'll remember that in 1968 it became available for some 396 V-8's only. Now you could get it even with a 6. Actually there were two Turbo Hydra-Matics, the M-38 and the M-40 or, in more familiar terms, the 350 and 400 units.

Torque-Drive was continued, again for 6-cylinder cars only.

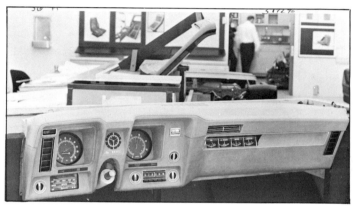

Camaro's '69 instrument panel went to square dials. Studies above and at right show evolution.

Houndstooth upholstery for 1969 came in black, white, yellow, and orange. Folding rear seatback option (not shown) continued, but Strato-back didn't.

Gauges differed but 1969 Camaro now shared panel housing with Chevy II. Clock fit into central square but could also be combined with 8000-rpm tach.

Option package envisioned for early 1970 production was called Berlinetta. Striping on vinyl roof ran counter to body striping. Another idea put forth: protruding driving lamps (inset) beneath integrated Endura bumper.

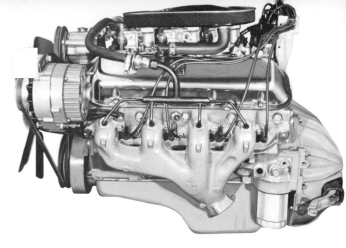

Chevrolet built 50 Camaro ZL-1's to qualify for NHRA drag racing. They all had aluminum 425-bhp 427 V-8 with triple 2-barrel carburetion. Two ZL-1's were dolled up by Design Staff for the enjoyment of Chevrolet executives. One such ZL-1 is pictured above, with its Corvette-derived V-8 shown at top right.

Editors of Sports Car Graphic borrowed race-prepared 1969 Camaro for extended test, found the car good for 143 but impractical at supermarket.

Unchanged from 1969, early '70 Camaros sold over 50,000 before new 1970½ models came out. Rally Sport's headlights had shine-through glass louvers so *oncoming drivers could see both lamps if doors froze shut. Included in RS package were headlight washers, available optionally for all '69-70 Camaros.*

THE YEAR 1969 HAD BEGUN with the 210-bhp 327 as the Camaro's standard V-8, same as 1967-68, and quite a few '69's were sold with 327's, now called the LF-3. But on Feb. 14 of that year, Chevrolet decided to replace the base 327 with the 307-cid V-8. So the 307 came in at mid-year and the LF-3 327 dropped quietly into the past.

Meanwhile, the 4-barrel 327 (L-30) had already been replaced by a new 350, the L-65, which in time would become the Camaro's base V-8 itself. Both the 307 and the new 350 meant slight decreases in horsepower when compared with the engines they superseded.

The 302 Camaro Z-28 engine took on 4-bolt mains for 1969, and now the 350's got them also. In addition, all 1969 small-block V-8's included thicker bulkheads and main-bearing caps, the bulkheads being completely filled and fully machined. These engines also got longer attaching bolts for better stress distribution. All in all, they were considerably stronger than the already-strong '68 blocks.

There were two types of ram-air induction systems for the 1969 Camaro. First, there was a new special hood with rear-facing inlet. A cold-air duct underneath the hood mated to the aircleaner via big, soft rubber gaskets for either single- or twin-carb installations. Then carried over from 1967-68 was the dealer-installed cowl plenum ram-air kit that cost $106 and came with a special aircleaner and adapter for the firewall plenum chamber. By blocking off the ventilator section of the cowl, installing this kit, and connecting the new chamber to the aircleaner by a rubber sleeve, you had a complete cold induction system without the special hood.

Standard for the 302 and 350-/375-bhp 396's was a new chambered dual exhaust system. You could get it optionally for the 325-horse 396 as well. Chevrolet also chucked the previous and rather balky Muncie floorshift levers for 4-speed manual gearboxes and began installing Hurst linkage and shifters instead. The Hurst system worked a lot better.

THE 1969 CAMARO RACKED UP another SCCA Trans-Am championship that season—its second in a row. The car also paced the '69 Indy 500 for the second time in three years and became NASCAR'S official pace car for its eight major stock-car races. It won CAR & DRIVER's 1969 readers' poll as the year's best sporty car, and Chevrolet sold more Camaros than ever before.

One reason for the high sales figure was the fact that Chevy continued the '69 Camaro well into 1970. Since the second-generation body style wasn't introduced until late Feb. 1970, many Camaros with the appearance of '69's were registered as 1970 models. Unofficial figures put the number of 1970-produced '69's at 53,526 units.

There were no visible differences in those 1970 carryover models; they look exactly like '69's. But their vehicle identification numbers (VIN) contained a zero as the sixth digit instead of the 9 that designated 1969. For example, a 1969 V-8-engined Camaro's VIN number would read 124379, whereas the same car built as 1970 model would have the beginning digits 124370.

Rumor had it that Chevrolet was going to put several ultra-high-performance V-8's into the 1969 Camaro, notably 427's from the Corvette; i.e. the L-72 and L-88 versions. However, no Corvette 427 was ever *factory* installed in a Camaro.

Instead, a limited-production build of 50 Camaros was made in 1969 with the *aluminum-block* 427, dubbed the ZL-1. This, according to Chevrolet production promotion engineer Vince Piggins, became COPO 9567. COPO stands for Central Office Production Order and designates an item that's produced in very limited quantity for very special customers.

"The COPO contained the all-aluminum 427 V-8," states Piggins, "plus other selected options including the cold-air hood. It carried a suggested list price of $8581.60 and was available in the base coupe only. There was no external identification of the 427."

This batch of 50 Camaro ZL-1's was intended primarily for drag racing. Horsepower nominally rated 425 but was much higher, and the car qualified for the National Hot Rod Association's A/Stock and A/Stock Automatic classes.

The ZL-1 proved a delight not only to serious drag racers but to several young management people in Chevrolet's downtown offices in Detroit. The story goes that these Chevy execs used to take a couple of ZL-1 Camaros out on Woodward Av. during their lunch breaks and dust off everything in sight.

Dealers and private individuals regularly installed L-72 and L-88 Corvette 427's in Camaros, and a couple of auto magazines were lent ultra-high-performance '69's for evaluation that year. SPORTS CAR GRAPHIC, edited by Trans-Am racer Jerry Titus for a time, lived with a street-driveable (but barely) $10,000 Z-28 with full roll cage and an engine that would hardly idle below 3000 rpm. SCG reported that this car was no less comfortable than a Model A Ford but that its 143-mph top speed didn't make it practical for trips to the supermarket.

CAR & DRIVER borrowed a different '69 coupe for a 3-month extended evaluation. This car, dubbed "Blue Maxi" and "Z-29," carried the 1970½ Camaro's 350-cid V-8, a slightly detuned version of the Corvette LT-1. C&D accessorized it to a fare thee well, let Penske tune it, and enjoyed the car tremendously.

Chapter Six

The Z-28's - Legends in

IF ONE MAN ALONE deserves credit for the Camaro Z-28, it's Vincent W. Piggins. Vince not only thought up the Z-28 but convinced Chevrolet management to put it into production so the car could be homologated and raced in SCCA's (Sports Car Club of America's) then-new Trans-Am sedan series.

In fact, without Vince's prodding, the SCCA might never have continued Trans-Am sedan competition at all. It was only after Piggins assured SCCA officials that Chevrolet would lend its support that a racing schedule materialized for 1967.

Vince, who's been a Chevrolet engineer since 1956 and who was *the* man behind the Hudson Hornet's NASCAR championships in the early 1950's, explains the Z-28's creation with these words:

"After Ford released the Mustang, they had about two years on us before Chevrolet could get the Camaro into the 1967 product line. I felt in my activity, which deals with product promotion and how to get the most promotional mileage from a car from the performance standpoint, that we needed to develop a performance image for the Camaro that would be superior to the Mustang's.

"Along comes SCCA in creating the Trans-Am sedan racing class for professional drivers in 1966, aimed at the 1967 season. I made it a point to have several discussions with SCCA officials—notably Jim Kaser, John Bishop, and Tracy Byrd—and one thing led to another. I suggested a vehicle that would fit this class and, I believe—supported by what Chevrolet might do with the Camaro—it gave them heart to push ahead and make up the rules, regulations, and so forth for the Trans-Am series. I feel this was really the creation of the Trans-Am as we know it."

All this took place in mid-1966, several months before the Camaro actually came out. The series was going to

be open to all American and European production sport sedans, FIA International Sporting Code, Chapter IV, Touring Cars, Group II, Appendix J. Rules held competitors to a 116-inch wheelbase maximum and 305 cid engine displacement, with only limited modifications. The rule, then as now, required a 1000 production minimum to be built by the end of any model year.

This was "sedan racing," mind you, and what qualified the Camaro and all ponycars as "sedans" was the fact that they had rear seats. And although Chevrolet sold only 602 Z-28's during 1967, they met the 1000 production rule by homologating the 350-cid Camaro under FIA Group I rules and then qualifying the same basic vehicle with the Z-28 *option* under Group II.

NOW ON AUG. 17, 1966," continues Piggins, "I put together a memo to my boss, W.T. Barwell, that laid out the basic idea of the Z-28, although, of course, it wasn't called that then. We didn't name the car until several months later, but I'll get into that in a moment.

"This memo went out to engineers Alex Mair and Don McPherson, sales manager Bob Lund, Joe Pike in sale promotion, and C.C. Jakust. I said, in effect, that SCCA sedan racing was becoming increasingly popular and would blossom into even bigger things with the advent of the short-wheelbase, Mustang-type ponycar.

"My proposal went on that since our projected engine lineup for the 1967 Camaro had no V-8 smaller than the 327, and since we were above the 5000cc (305-cid) SCCA displacement limit for Class A sedans, we ought to take a high-performance version of the old 283 and wrap an option package around it to make it competitive within SCCA. You'll remember that the Barracuda was running a 273 V-8 at that time, and the Mustang's competitive engine was the 289. So our high-performance 283 would certainly have been right in there."

The key portions of Piggins' Aug. 17 memo said, "A new 283 high-performance engine plus other relative driveline and chassis items will provide performance and handling characteristics superior to either Mustang or Barracuda. To aid in the merchandising of this vehicle, certain other embellishments have been included to make the overall vehicle immediately identifiable and distinctive. The sales department anticipates a volume of 10,000 such vehicles could be sold in 1967."

Piggins now resumes his narrative: "My initial proposal suggested we use the 283 V-8 plus the F-41 optional suspension, with heavy-duty front coils and multi-leaf rear springs. I also requested the J-52 front disc brakes with J-65 metallic linings for the rear drums, the 11-inch clutch from the 396 V-8, the close-ratio 4-speed with 2.20 low, a brand-new steering gear with a 24:1 overall ratio, Corvette 15 x 6 wheels with 7.75 tires, and a special reworked hood to provide functional air intake. There were other modifications called for as well, and I suggested we make the package available only in the Camaro coupe, not the convertible, and that the Z-22 Rally Sport option form part of the equipment for this car. Now not all this equipment went into the production Z-28 automobile, but those were the initial parts called for."

PIGGINS GOT PERMISSION to have a pre-production Z-28 prototype built to these initial specifications, and during a "show-and-tell" session to top management at the GM Proving Grounds on Oct. 4, 1966, he trotted out the car.

One of his first passengers in the as-yet-unnamed Z-28 was Chevrolet's new general manager, Elliott M. (Pete) Estes. The ride didn't come until just before noon. After some full-throttle acceleration runs and a

their Own Time

Steve Kelly wrings out first 302-cid Z-28 at Riverside introduction in Nov. 1966.

Mandatory front discs for '67 Z-28 complemented 15-in. Rally wheels with "Disc Brakes" on spinners.

While hood and deck striping came standard with Z-28, RS equipment and D-80 spoiler didn't. Both are visible here, plus optional bumper guards and vinyl top. Early Z's didn't carry 302 front-fender emblems.

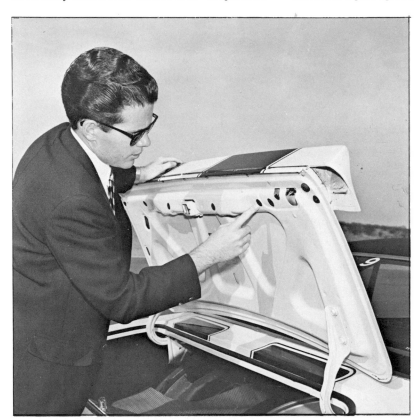

Fiberglass spoiler aided high-speed traction by giving downforce at rear, yet it weighed so little that trunk countersprings could be set to lift decklid easily.

Cowl plenum chamber let cold air into aircleaner via big rubber duct. Headers cost $200-$300 additional, came in trunk for dealer or customer installation.

Rally wheels for 1968, like Vette's, looked different from '67's because of heftier fluted spinners.

few dives through a slalom course, Piggins let Estes take the wheel.

"Estes was quite impressed with the performance of this 283-engined vehicle," recalls Piggins, "and as I explained to him what we planned to do to capture the Trans-Am championship and to produce a good performance image for the Camaro, it didn't take much convincing for Pete to see what I was aiming toward.

"The only thing. . ." continues Vince, "while we were driving the car, I mentioned that we'd put the 283 into it because we'd built that size engine before. But I suggested when we got back to the starting pad that it might be a lot better to take the 327 block and put the 283 crank into it, giving us a 4 x 3 bore and stroke. That would put displacement at 302.4 cid, just under the SCCA's 305 limit.

"So Pete immediately agreed, especially being an engineer and knowing the potential this car could have. Estes walked over to engineers Alex Mair and Don McPherson and said, 'Let's release this package and develop a 302 engine to go with it.'

"That was really the start of the Z-28, and we proceeded to homologate that vehicle with the FIA as of Jan. 1, 1967 as a Group II car."

BUT EVEN BEFORE that could happen, Chevrolet built up a prototype 302-engined showcar and actually displayed it for the motoring press at a special

For 1968, 302 or Z-28 emblems appeared on front fenders. RS grille (shown) took on silver-painted horizontal bars. Heavy-duty F-41 suspension kept Z-28's flat on most corners but wasn't up to all-out racing.

Stark in its black Rally Sport attire, Z-28 could be ordered with many more racing options for 1968.

Optional 2x4 manifold with twin Holleys boosted top speed but wasn't recommended for street because it idled poorly below 3000 rpm. Dressup for '68 included chromed rocker covers, oil-filler pipe, aircleaner.

Generously vented 11¾-inch rear discs gave excellent fade resistance and weren't affected by water.

Z-28's had to drag race in NHRA and AHRA classes that pitted them against cars with much larger engines, yet Z's generally fured well in 1320 competition.

Car Life's Allan Girdler tested 2x4 Z 28, turned quarter mile in 15.12 sec at 94.8 mph, with a top speed of 133 mph and no fade from the 4-wheel discs.

Vince Piggins, father of the Z-28, reports that only about 200 sets of 4-wheel disc brakes were sold. They cost over $500. Most went to Trans-Am racers.

Front air dam, designed by Paul van Valken-burgh, became a popular Z-28 accessory in '68-69.

preview. This preview was held at Riverside International Raceway in California in Nov. 1966 at the windup of the ARRC events there.

Walt Mackenzie, who was Chevrolet's public-relations liaison at the time, set up a special trackside tent at Riverside, with a technical news handout. This showed the Camaro coupe with what was called simply Regular Production Option (RPO) Z-28. The magazine writers and editors were allowed to drive this first Z-28. To a man, they loved the car, and MOTOR TREND, SPORTS CAR GRAPHIC, HOT ROD, CAR & DRIVER, ROAD & TRACK, and several others published rave reviews soon afterward.

Some people believed that the Z in Z-28 stood for *Zora,* as in Zora Arkus-Duntov, the Corvette engineer. Not so. Piggins had put a name on the original 283 prototype before he presented it at the October show-and-tell. The name Piggins had chosen was *Cheetah.* But Vince took that handmade decal off the car at the last moment, muttering, ''Well, a name is a name is a name,'' and the coupe Estes drove carried no designation at all.

''There wasn't any suggestion of *what* we were going to call this car,'' notes Piggins. ''When it came down to having to decide, somebody just said, 'Hey, it's option RPO Z-28; let's call it Z-28!' So the name just grew from there. The graphics people did things with the Z, and that's how the designation stuck. The car got its name from the actual option number.''

Ironically, Z-27 is the RPO number for the early Camaro Super Sport package, and Z-28 simply followed it sequentially. RPO Z-29 apparently hasn't been taken yet, but perhaps Chevrolet is keeping it in reserve for some future Z-28 successor.

Y OU'RE AWARE, of course, that Camaro Z-28's won the Trans-Am championship two years running—1968 and 1969. The resulting publicity helped Camaro sales immeasurably.

Racing also transformed the early Camaro from a me-too car that followed the Mustang into an image car that consistently came in ahead of Mustangs on the track. So the Z-28 made a big difference in the Camaro's early sales record.

Not that the Z-28 you could buy over the counter in 1967-68-69 was anywhere near the same car that won SCCA championships, because the Z-28's that Roger Penske, Mark Donohue, Smokey Yunick, Ronny Bucknum, Jerry Thompson, Tony DeLorenzo, and other professionals ran were honed to an incredibly fine edge. More about that in the next chapter.

But RPO Z-28 did at least form the basis of their cars, and as people like Penske and Donohue learned more about what they needed to win races, Chevrolet began making and cataloguing the parts. These parts immediately became available to everyone.

Specifications and details for the 1967-69 production Z-28's are given on pp. 80-81 in our *Z-28 Comparator.* Horsepower during those years was listed at 290 at 5800 rpm *nominal.* It's important to keep that word *nominal* in mind, because it means the 290 figure was just something somebody plugged into Chevy's spec sheets. It might just as well have been 300 or 350 or 400 bhp. Most, if not all, Z-28 302's put out more than 290 bhp and 290 foot-pounds of torque at 4200 rpm.

Actual horsepower depended a lot on which intake and exhaust manifolds you chose, which carburetor(s), and what internal mods you pursued. No actual dyno figures were ever released by Chevrolet for the 302-cid Z-28 engine, but the auto magazines didn't hesitate to speculate. Their estimates ranged from a realistic 350

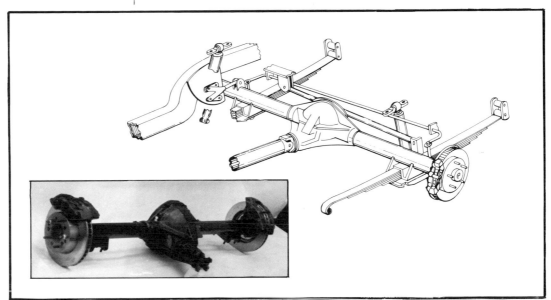

Rear discs from Corvette became a service option for 1968, then an RPO for '69. Axle with traction bars served Trans-Am racers, yet anyone could order it. All post-'67 302's carried multi-leaf rear springs.

Beginning in 1969, Z-28's 302 V-8 got 4-bolt mains. High-performance 350's and 396's already had them. Factory rated Z-28's horsepower at a conservative 290 while in actuality it put out more like 340-360 bhp.

bhp in ROAD & TRACK to 370-plus in SPORTS CAR GRAPHIC to 400 bhp in CAR LIFE. All-out, blueprinted racing versions, like those built by Traco and Yunick, probably delivered in the neighborhood of 450 bhp, which took some heavy tinkering to pull from 302 cid and still expect reliability.

One of the amazing facets of the first-generation Z-28 was its warranty. Chevrolet didn't flinch and applied the same 2-year/24,000-mile warranty to the Z-28 automobile as a whole and its 5-year/50,000-mile warranty to the powertrain. That went beyond expectation and contrary to the practice of warranties for most high-performance packages.

CHEVROLET DIDN'T ESPECIALLY encourage the purchase of Z-28's by private individuals at

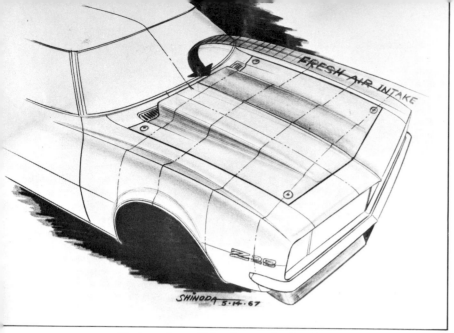

Designer Larry Shinoda conceived cold-air hood for '69 Camaro in May 1967 at Piggins' request. Many were made of fiberglass.

High-pressure area exists at base of Camaro's windshield; also SCCA rules no longer allowed underhood cold-air systems. Cold-air hood was available for any '69, not just Z.

Several different types of internal ducts and seals were used with cold-air hoods, depending on engine and carburetion. Two are seen with dual 4-barrel setups.

For the 1970½ Z-28, Chevrolet introduced an all-new Rally wheel with black center and 7-inch rim.

The 1970½ Camaro Z-28 has been called by Chevrolet engineers "the least compromised of the series." Its 350-cid V-8 delivered more power with less strain than before; its body was quieter and more comfortable.

Derived from Corvette LT-1 (shown with ignition shielding), Camaro's 1970½ V-8 put out 360 bhp without fuss or temperament. Despite performance, engine had reliability.

First Z-28 to be released for evaluation by the press, this coupe created an immediate sensation at Riverside preview in Nov. 1966. It lacked the 302 emblems on front fenders but carried Rally wheels, spoiler, and paint stripes common to most 1967 Z-28's.

Camaros successfully campaigned the nation's drag strips, although Z-28's were often put into classes that ran much bigger engines than 302. Phil Pyle's F/Modified Production '67 took runner-up in the 1976 Gaternationals after a long series of class wins.

Stock Z-28 for 1970½ remains one of the world's finest all-around street machines.

After its 2-year vacation, the Z-28 reappeared as a 1977½ model at the Chicago Auto Show on Feb. 26. Lacking some of its earlier steam, the new Z-28 came through as a handling package. Specific goodies included beefed suspension, steel-belted radials, fast steering, and 185-bhp 350 V-8. Non-California cars carried Borg-Warner T-10 4-speed gearbox and 11-inch clutch.

Two spoilers were offered for 1970½-71: low D-80 (right) and COPO type that borrowed Firebird center.

Finned covers on 1970½ Z-28 had internal galleries that distributed oil more evenly to rockers.

Second-generation Camaro Z-28's came with rear stabilizer bars, but 4-wheel discs were dropped.

first and didn't start actually advertising the Camaro Z-28 until 1968.

The first 25 Z-28's were built between Dec. 29, 1966 and Jan. 12, 1967. These went strictly to favored dealers, mostly for reworking as all-out competition cars. Z-28 #1 was shipped to Aero Chevrolet in Alexandria, Va., where it was groomed as Johnny Moore's entry in the Daytona 24-hour Continental. Cars #2, #3, and #4 went to Yenko Chevrolet, Canonsburg, Pa., for driver Ben Poster, also for Daytona.

Seattle dealer Alan Green received Z-28's #5 through #7, reselling one to a Daytona, Fla., dealer, one to a local Northwest dealer, and the third to a local customer. That means that Z-28 #7 was probably the first to fall into private hands. Many people believe that the 1967 Z-28 didn't debut until late in the model year, but that simply isn't true. A few were in private hands by Feb. 1, 1967.

Ron Tonkin, a Chevrolet dealer in Portland, Ore., ordered Z-28 #8 and placed it on his Beaver Racing Team, which ran mostly West Coast events. After careful preparation, it was involved in an accident while being trailered to its first race. That ended its competition career.

Nickey Chevrolet in Chicago, which went into racing in a big way (e.g. putting 427's into Camaros for the dragstrip), took delivery of Z-28's #9-#10-#11. Two of these ran at Daytona along with the Aero and Yenko cars.

Roger Penske acquired the 12th Z-28, his friend George Wintersteen picking it up at the factory on Jan. 10, 1967 and driving it back to Penske's Chevrolet agency in Reading, Pa. Penske immediately tore down the car and sent the engine to Traco in his push toward entering Daytona.

The next eight Z's went to a variety of customers, including three shipped to other GM divisions and one sold to a GM Proving Grounds engineer named David D. Horchler. Car #21 was delivered to stunt driver Joie Chitwood in Tampa, Fla. Chitwood raced the car and has subsequently used Camaros in all his thrill shows ever since.

FOR THE AVERAGE private citizen to buy a street version of the Z-28 took quite some doing at first. Dealers weren't knowledgeable about these special-order cars, so customers needed plenty of patience, know-how, a sympathetic dealer, and some extra dollars.

If you'd been interested in ordering a Z-28 in, say, 1968, you'd be faced with the following procedure. You'd first order a conventional Camaro 6-cylinder coupe at the base price of $2694. (Prices given here were current in early 1968). Add to that the Z-28 package, consisting of the 302 V-8, F-41 heavy-duty suspension, special 15 x 6-inch Corvette Rally wheels and E70-15 Goodyear Wide Tread GT tires, Z-28 paint striping on the hood and rear deck, quicker-than-normal N-44 non-power steering option, and the 302 front-fender emblems.

But *with* the $400.25 Z-28 basic package, you also had to order two specified *mandatory* options: front disc brakes (RPO J-52) with vacuum assist (J-50) at $100.10, and one of three available 4-speed transmissions (at least $184.35). So right away you were starting off with a package that added $684.70 to the base price of a Camaro coupe (Z-28 convertibles were never offered).

You might further want to toss in goodies like the RS package (RPO Z-22; $105.35), the tack-on fiberglass rear spoiler (D-80; $32.68), Positraction (G-80; $42.15), the still-quicker power steering (N-40; $84.30), and the sintered metallic rear linings (J-65; $37.90). A set of fabricated steel-tubing headers came from the factory for about $200 extra but were supplied inside the trunk and had to be dealer-installed. The twin 4-barrel manifold with dual Holley 600-cfm carbs added another $500 or so and again had to be dealer-installed. Finally, the cowl plenum ram-air system came to $79.

The Z-28 arrived with stock exhaust manifolds, and it was up to the individual buyer to arrange for headers if he wanted them. In addition to those supplied ''in the trunk,'' shops and dealers sold a variety of others.

The 2x4 carburetion setup wasn't really intended for street driving. It gave a very rough idle and actually accounted for slower 0-60-mph times than the normal 4-barrel Holley. It was only above 3000 rpm that the 2x4 came into its own.

The JL-8 disc brakes, which put one 11.75-inch rotor at each wheel, cost $500.30 additional when introduced late in 1968 as an RPO for the 1969 model year. Four-wheel discs were available for all '69 Camaros, not just the Z-28, although only about 200 sets were built. CAR LIFE tested the 4-wheel disc setup and reported no fade and no loss of control after repeated panic stops. ''The four-wheel discs make a good braking system better,'' said CL. The driver could push the brakes very hard without locking the wheels, and the decelerometer read 30 ft./sec./sec.

FOR THE 1970 SEASON, SCCA rules were changed to allow destroking for the first time. Up until 1970, no factory engine could be destroked to fit the 305-cid SCCA limit, which left Chrysler Corp. out of the running. Chrysler had only the 273 and 318 V-8's, with nothing in between.

In order to let the Plymouth Barracuda and Dodge Challenger compete in Trans-Am sedan racing, a meeting was held between SCCA officials and members of several factory performance staffs, notably from GM, Ford, and AMC. At this meeting, it was agreed to allow destroking so Chrysler Corp. might compete with the rest.

Once the new rules came into effect, there was no need for Chevrolet to hang onto the 302, because the 350 could be downsized exactly the same way the 327 had been. The 350 had the same bore as the 327, so the

The 1970½ Z-28 could again be combined with RS. Corvette-inspired tail lamps blended into Kamm chop.

The 1971 Camaro remained almost unchanged, although the comfortable, all-foam, low-back seats gave way to high-back versions of Vega buckets. RS grille (shown) sported urethane frame, rubber center bar.

You'd again be hard-pressed to identify RS-optioned 1972 Z-28 (shown), but non-RS Camaros with full front bumpers had coarser grille mesh than before.

The 1972 models dropped low spoiler, made front air dam a part of the D-80 option. Hood and decklid stripes were not a standard part of Z-28 package.

crankshaft from the 283-cid V-8 fit just as before.

Thus in the interest of deproliferation, the 350 became the Z-28's new engine for 1970½. But it wasn't just any 350, nor was it just the 350 that had powered Camaros before.

The 1970½ Z-28 350 turned out to be essentially the LT-1 introduced in the Corvette that year. Chevrolet rated the Camaro's version at 10 bhp less than the Vette's 370. Torque, though, was the same in both: 380 foot-pounds.

According to many writers, engineers, and Camaro owners, the 1970½ Z-28, with its new engine and new body style, beat the socks off any Z-28 before it and all of those that followed. The LT-1 engine proved more tractable, more reliable, less temperamental, had more torque off the line, and generally out-performed the more highly stressed 302 in every way.

Furthermore, the 1970½ model represented the first Z-28 to come stock with front disc brakes, front and rear anti-roll bars, the less understeering new front

suspension, more comfortable seats, plus the much better insulated and quieter new body. Turbo Hydra-Matic became a Z-28 option for the first time, and there was little difference in performance between the automatic and the 4-speed.

Chevy engineer Jim Ingle once remarked that, "The 1970½ Z-28 was the least compromised car we ever sold." He's undoubtedly right that the '70½ Z-28 was a lot less compromised in terms of stress than the 1967-69 models, fine as they were. But anyone who's pulled up

In 1972, Camaro designers took a company car out of service and began to play with bold Z-28 graphics. Randy Wateen refined this theme for 1974 decals.

Aluminum bumpers arrived for 1974 along with emissions restrictions that put a lid on performance. Chevy suspended Z-28 production at end of model year.

to a red light in one of the first-generation Z-28's, with their high-idling 302 loping and tugging at the leash, can appreciate the new smoothness and silence of the 350's.

And yet as pointed out in our *Z-28 Comparator* (pp. 80-81), the 350 still came with 4-bolt mains and a forged-steel crank, same as before. Main- and rod-bearing dimensions remained unchanged from the 302 (2.450 and 2.099 inches respectively). Pistons and rods were straight out of Chevrolet's Corvette high-performance bin, with the TRW-made pistons very

similar to the 302's: same dome configuration, same 11:1 compression ratio.

The new cam grind was a bit milder than the 302's, with less lift, less intake duration, and reduced overlap. Intake duration fell 29 degrees short of the 302's normal street cam. But the 350 still had mechanical lifters.

A new, lower aluminum manifold for the 1970½ again mounted a 780-800-cfm Holley 4-barrel. The 1969 dual-quad manifold was still listed for '70½ as a dealer accessory, but it needed a revised hood to accommodate

the twin carburetors. Most post-1970 Trans-Am Camaros still ran the 2 x 4 setup.

Vince Piggins states that a steel, cold-air-ducted hood was available for 1970½ and that Chevrolet earlier had tried a Vette-type scoop hood for that year. But John DeLorean, Chevrolet's new general manager, didn't like that hood, calling it a "coffin." Also, SCCA rules for 1970 didn't allow a raised hood design. "So we built an internal cold-air hood—an internally ducted design that picked up cold air ahead of the radiator. That was the

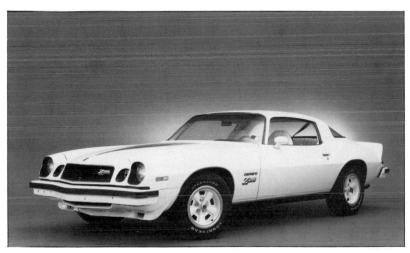

Z-28 made its return as a 1977½ model with emphasis on looks and handling. Suspension refinements put Z into league with the finest European GT cars.

Camaros kept the same basic instrument panel from 1970½ through 1978, but Z-28 took on working gauges and simulated string-wrapped wheel rim for '78.

first time we ever used that innovation in the Camaro.''

The 1970½ Z-28 shared its overall body configuration with the rest of that year's Camaros, but several distinctions set the Z-28 apart. Wide stripes on the hood and deck made the Z stand out as before, as did two different deck spoilers that year.

Throughout the 1970½ and '71 seasons, the Z-28 package included a standard, one-piece, low-profile rear spoiler very much like the 1967-69's. This low spoiler, still designated RPO D-80 at the time, bolted to the decklid and overlapped the rear fenders slightly on each side.

Then on Apr. 20, 1970, an entirely different optional spoiler came on the scene—the same tall, 3-piece spoiler that's still used today. Temporarily coded COPO 9796 so it didn't conflict with RPO D-80, this larger spoiler was actually the Firebird spoiler, but Chevrolet designers added different end caps. There's a story behind this.

"We needed a bigger spoiler for the new Z-28,'' says Vince Piggins, ''but new tooling would have been quite expensive, with a lead time of at least six months. So we borrowed the Firebird's center section. John DeLorean got permission from Pontiac general manager Jim McDonald, and Camaro designers did individualize the end caps, but the center section was and is strictly Firebird.''

AS MUSCLE CARS faded year by year with tighter emission and noise regulations, the Z-28 inevitably retrenched. Never again would a Z-28 approach the golden age of the first-generation 302's nor the 1970½ 350 V-8's.

Compression ratios for all 1971 GM engines were mandated by the corporation at 8.5:1 maximum so they could burn unleaded fuel. The only Chevrolet engines to escape this edict were the Z-28 and a few Corvettes, which ended up with 9.0:1 c.r. through 1974.

For 1972, the Z-28's horsepower rating slid to 255 net, then 245 in 1973-74. Solid lifters gave way to a hydraulic cam for 1973, although the same high engine quality persisted—the 4-bolt mains, baffled pan, big-valve heads, etc. And for 1973, due to the addition of EGR (exhaust gas recirculation), the high-rise aluminum intake manifold succumbed to a conventional cast-iron one that mounted a Rochester Quadra-jet instead of the previous high-performance Holley. It marked the end of that era.

In 1972, the optional D-80 spoiler package began to include a front air dam, and variable-ratio power steering gave way to a straight power-steering system with a 16:1 ratio. The good, all-foam Camaro seats introduced in 1970½ had been replaced by modified Vega units during 1971, with an optional seatback tilt/adjuster (AN-6) added. The standard Z-28 rear stabilizer bar for 1972 took on a little more heft, and the car's shocks came in for a slight revaluing.

For 1973, the price of the Z-28 option dropped abruptly. It had been as high as $786.75 in 1971, but for

While 1979 Camaro instrument panel had been redesigned, it kept the same gauge cluster as before. Seats were made more comfortable, with rears separated by tunnel. Power steering, brakes became standard.

1973 the price went down to $502.05. Was this an effort to spark sales? If so, the price reduction probably wasn't necessary, because Camaros were selling briskly in 1973 after the nearly fatal 174-day UAW strike at the Norwood, Ohio, F-body assembly plant. The strike all but ended the Camaro's life, and it did have something to do with the Z-28's discontinuance after 1974.

For 1974, the big Camaro news involved going with aluminum bumpers, adding the revised nose and grille and wrap-around tail lamps. Along with those items, the Z-28 got big hood and deck lettering, the bold graphics created by designer Randy Wateen.

This 1974 Z-28 decal, by an error in printing, was supposed to have see-through sections with white surrounds. This way it would complement any paint color. But as it turned out, the intended clear sections were also printed in white. That means that only white 1974 Z-28's looked the way they were intended.

The Arab oil embargo of Dec. 1973, combined with rising insurance rates for high-performance cars, plus government-mandated noise and emissions standards, made the outlook for future Z-28's bleak indeed. General Motors decided to drop the Z-28 after the 1974 model year rather than dilute it still further. Designer Jerry Palmer sums it up by saying, "Chevrolet took the position that we'd rather kill the car now before it died a slow, lingering death. So we stopped the Z-28 after the 1974 model year."

DURING THE Z-28's HIATUS, Camaros ran on the track as they never had before. Penske Racing had decided to switch from expensive Porsches to Camaros in the IROC series. Converted to run just as fast as the Porsches, the 15 IROC Camaros for the 1974-75 season cost about half as much as the German cars.

Camaros have continued as IROC cars (see *The Camaro Goes Racing,* next chapter) since that day, and it's logical to assume that the Camaro's good publicity in racing contributed to the Z-28's return in Feb. 1977. People wanted a car like the ones they saw on TV broadcasts of the IROC series, so Chevy revived the Z as a mid-year 1977 model.

But instead of resurrecting the Z-28 as a simple decal package—or as the muscle car it had been long before—Chevrolet decided to bring it back as a *handler.* The 1977½ Z-28 represented much more a suspension and steering package than one intended for brute strength.

Engineer Jack W. Turner, Jr., working under Camaro chief engineer Tom R. Zimmer, had responsibility for the Z-28's mechanical revisions for '77½. Turner's group, which enjoyed a reputation as corporate suspension doctors, had just finished suspension-tuning GM's full-sized 1977 cars when it got the Z-28 assignment in the summer of 1976.

"We decided to make a road machine out of the Z-28, and not a dragster. Emissions and fuel requirements

The Z-28 lost 10 more of its horsepower for 1979, was now down to 175. Ironically, the carburetor took in cold air above radiator. Most late-model Z's were ordered with air conditioning and automatic trans.

Impeccable road manners, mean and powerful appearance have created strong surge in demand for '78-79 Z-28's. It's unlikely that the basic body will change before 1982, making this one of GM's longest runs.

Understated yet unignorable Z abandoned bright-work when Camaro went to soft nose and tail.

restricted what could be done to the engine, so we concentrated on handling. We wanted to make the vehicle feel that it was positively with you all the time—that the steering wheel was glued to the road without a rubber-band in between.''

Turner's group tautened up the front and rear springs, increased the size of the front anti-roll bar, then softened the rear bar and put on larger wheels and tires. Front spring rates went from 300 lb./in. in 1974 to 365 for 1977½-78 in the Z-28. Rear rates rose to 127 lb./in. from 89-99. The previous 1.0-inch front stabilizer was replaced by a 1.2-inch bar, and its rear mate was slimmed to 0.55 inch from 1974's 0.6875 inch. Front shock valving stayed the same (and the same as the optional F-41 suspension's), but the rear was slightly revised to go with the thinner anti-roll bar.

''Working out suspension details,'' says Turner, ''involves a combination of computer analysis and cut-and-try. The final judgments, though, are seat-of-the-pants. We had a number of ways to go. We could put roll stiffness into the vehicle with just stabilizer bars, but then it's not too good on tramp input. If we try to go up in spring rates to increase roll stiffness, we can get to a point where we lose an awful lot of isolation.

''We tried to pick a happy medium between going up in spring rates and still not having to add homungous stabilizer bars. We tried to balance the system so the car could go over road undulations and go into corners with chatter bumps so that the suspension would allow the tires to envelope some of that roughness instead of skidding across the tops. That means a lot of refinement between the shock valving, spring rate, and stabilizer-bar rate. You've got to balance the whole package together.''

Turner's people also speeded up the steering ratio

Details, decals made no secret of '79's identity.

from the previous overall ratio of 14.3:1 to 13.02:1. Power assist was still standard, but the variable-ratio feature was eliminated. Quite a bit of time was spent on tire selection, too. The final choice was a steel-belted GR70-15, which also turned out to be the Corvette tire. These mounted on new 15 x 7-inch Z-28 wheels.

Horsepower in the 1977½ Z-28 came in at 185 bhp net, with 280 ft./lb. of torque—a low but ample figure. Gone were the 4-bolt mains, the forged crank, and any vestige of a long-duration cam.

The Z-28's 4-speed was now a Borg-Warner T-10 with a nicely refined shifter. Turbo Hydra-Matic became mandatory in California and much favored elsewhere. Axle ratios were chosen to complement the car's cornering ability.

"We got the vehicle very responsive and very close to neutral when you apply power," continues Jack Turner. "If you go around a corner under power, you end up with a nice neutral drift or you can even trick it into an oversteer if you want to."

Not only did the Z-28 now handle in the best GT tradition, it also looked good. The 1977½ graphics impressed everyone—the blacked-out paint highlighted with decal-trimmed wheel lip moldings and bold Z-28 signs front and rear, contrasting so beautifully with the tricolor tail-lamp ensemble: a striking car from any angle. Spoiler and air dam were now standard, and you had a choice of colors and comfort options.

"We were interested in putting together a quality, handling, durable machine. Throughout the whole program, cost wasn't the object as long as we had the pieces available," concludes Turner. And the pieces fit together remarkably well.

This basic Z-28 package continued in 1978-79, but the engine lost 10 bhp net in the latter year.

Extensive use of urethane, fiberglass, and plastic helped lighten 1979 Camaros. Soft face amounted to an end cap, with integrated grille and sugar scoops. Aluminum wheels for 1978-79 Z-28's came in anodized gold or silver.

Camaro Z-28

1967 Camaro Z-28 equipment & options

Engine: 302-cid V-8 made by installing 283 crank in 327 block for 4 x 3-inch bore and stroke. The 1967 Z-28 had 2-bolt mains. The Z-28 crank was forged steel instead of the more common nodular cast iron.

The Z-28 302 used Corvette L-79 big-port heads, with 11:1 c.r. and 2.0-inch intake valves, 1.6-inch exhaust. Standard 1967 Z-28 camshaft gave 346 degrees duration for both intake and exhaust, with 118 degrees of overlap. Solid lifters and 1.50:1 rockers provided 0.485-inch valve lift. Optional cams could be fitted.

Standard intake was an aluminum "tuned runner" manifold with 4-barrel, 780-800-cfm Holley. Transistor ignition with mechanical tach drive became a service-order part, with a special coil and advance curve. High-pressure oil pump and baffled pan standard. Five-bladed viscous fan and deep-groove double pulleys likewise. The Z-28 engine dressup kit included chromed rocker covers, chromed open-element aircleaner, bright oil filler tube and cap.

Optional under the hood: a cold-air ram induction system from an opening ahead of the cowl plenum chamber. A special aircleaner was linked to the cowl via a large duct. You could also order headers of various types, none factory installed (normal cast-iron manifolds were supplied on the engine), and you also had to put on your own twin exhausts and mufflers.

Clutch: 10.34-inch bent-finger unit.

Transmission: A 4-speed transmission became a mandatory option for the Z-28. Only the Muncie close-ratio with 2.20 low was available for the 1967 model year.

Rear axle: Standard Z-28 ratio was 3.73, with 3.07, 3.31, 3.55, 4.10, 4.56, and 4.88 optional. All could be had with Positraciton, but the last three had to be ordered with Positraction.

Brakes: The first Z-28 brakes were the 11-inch front discs (J-56) with vacuum assist (L-52). The calipers had one-inch-thick fiber insulators to keep heat away from the fluid, and the pads were the hard, racing type. Rear drums could be ordered with sintered metallic linings. In late 1967, Chevrolet re-machined the front calipers to accept Corvette pads. These had two retaining pins instead of the previous single pin, the idea being to keep the pads from cocking.

Front suspension: Standard F-41 heavy-duty springs and shock absorbers, with shot-peened ball studs.

Rear suspension: Special F-41 single-leaf springs, heavy-duty shocks, radius rod on right side of axle to counter wheel hop on acceleration.

Steering: Manual steering standard, with 24:1 ratio. Optional: power steering (N-40; $84.30) with 17.5:1 ratio and faster-ratio manual steering (20:1 gear with short spindle arms) at 17.9:1.

Wheels & tires: 15 x 6 slotted steel disc wheels (Corvette Rally type), Goodyear 7.35 x 15 2-ply nylon tires standard.

Special equipment included in the Z-28 package: "302" emblems on front fenders, specific paint striping for hood and deck. Optional: Rear spoiler (D-80; $32.68), Rally Sport group (Z-22; $105.35), tunnel console (D-55; $47.70), console instrument cluster (U-17; $79), and all normal Camaro options except SS package and those that conflict with Z-28 equipment.

1968 Camaro Z-28 equipment & options

Engine: Same as 1967, but 302's and 327's got bigger crankshaft bearing diameters: rod journals up .100 inch, mains up .150 and .160 inch for 1968. Options still included the cowl-plenum ram air. Also, a dealer-installed, aluminum, dual cross-ram, 4-barrel manifold with two 600-cfm Holleys became available in 1968 and could be connected to the cold-air induction system. This 2x4 wasn't recommended for the street.

Clutch, transmission, rear axle: Same as for 1967.

Brakes: Same mandatory power front-disc option as for 1967. Added as a service option were 4-wheel disc brakes toward the end of the model year. These had 11.75-inch Corvette rotors for a total swept area of 461.2 square inches and became RPO JL-8 for 1969.

Front suspension: Same as for 1967. A 1.0625-inch front anti-roll bar became optional to replace standard 0.6875-inch.

Rear suspension: New 5-leaf springs standard for Z-28, with staggered heavy-duty shocks. Radius rods removed from right side.

Steering: Fast (21.4:1) non-power steering standard; RPO N-44 faster-ratio (17.9:1) optional; others available with power.

Wheels & tires: Same 15 x 6-inch wheels with different trim rings and hubs (Corvette Rally type again); E70-15 Goodyear Wide Tread tires.

Special equipment: Many more all-out racing options available for 1968 than '67, including such things as special steering parts, different-rate front and rear springs, molded plastic bucket seats, front and rear spoilers, etc.

1969 Camaro Z-28 equipment & options

Mechanically, the 1969 Camaro Z-28 was identical to the 1968 model with these exceptions: 4-bolt mains for the 302 V-8, 4-wheel disc brakes became an RPO instead of a service option, 15 x 7-inch Rally wheels replaced 15 x 6-inchers. Tires: Firestone E70-15 Sports Car 200. And the cold-air hood with rear-facing scoop was added for 1969. Aluminum rocker covers optional.

1970½ Camaro Z-28 equipment & options

Engine: New 350-cid, 360-bhp V-8 derived from Corvette LT-1. Four-bolt mains, forged steel crank, TRW impact-extruded pistons, 11:1 c.r. Standard 1970½ cam was last year's optional cam, with 317-degree intake duration and 346-degree exhaust. Lift: 0.458 inches intake and exhaust.

Carburetion by Holley 780-cfm 4-barrel atop new high-rise aluminum manifold. Spark via aluminum single-point, vacuum-controlled distributor. Same high-performance oil pump, baffled pan, windage tray as in 302. Cast aluminum rocker covers with internal galleries. Twin-pulley fan drive. Mechanical valve lifters continued. Same heads and valve sizes as 302. Chrome dressup kit continued. Larger-capacity radiator. The 1970½ Z-28 package cost $572.95, with 4-speed or Turbo Hydra-Matic mandatory options.

Clutch: New 11-inch unit replaced 302's 10.34-inch disc.

Transmission: Mandatory choice of same Muncie 4-speeds as before, with beefed-up (2400-rpm-stall tor-

Comparator

que converter) Turbo Hydra-Matic optional—the first time an automatic transmission could be ordered in the Z-28.

Rear axle: Same as before, even to ratios. Positraction optional.

Brakes: 11-inch, vented, cast-iron front discs with vacuum assist standard. Rear 9.5-inch drums. Four-wheel disc brakes no longer offered.

Front suspension: Basically similar to previous Camaro's. Z-28 anti-roll bar 1.0-inch diameter instead of standard 0.6875-inch unit.

Rear suspension: RPO F-41 special suspension standard, including 5-leaf rear springs, 125 lb./in. spring rate, staggered heavy-duty shocks, link-type rear stabilizer bar.

Steering: Standard non-power steering ratio 18.8:1 or 4.1 turns lock to lock. Optional power steering came as variable-ratio at 14.3-10.9:1 for 2.3 turns lock to lock. Steering linkage now ahead of front axle.

Wheels & tires: 15 x 7 steel wheels, F60-15 fiberglass-belted tires standard.

Special equipment: Low-profile rear spoiler standard; 3-piece high spoiler (COPO 9796) available optionally after Apr. 20, 1970.

1971 Camaro Z-28 equipment & options

Engine: Same basic 350 as previously, but with compression ratio lowered from 11:1 to 9:1, resulting in 30 fewer horses and 20 fewer ft./lb. of torque. GM also began rating all engines in SAE net instead of gross horsepower. The Z-28 engine still had its solid-lifter cam, with the same 0.4850-inch lift. Durations identical to 1970½. Heftier engine mounts, bigger fuel filter, and H-D U-joints part of Z-28 package for 1971.

Other details: Steering ratios changed slightly for 1971. The 22.5:1 unassisted gear became standard, with variable-ratio power steering now at 15.5-11.8:1 for all Camaros—not quite so fast as before. 15 x 7-inch Trans-Am wheels standard. Z-28 option cost $786.75, and included power disc brakes.

1972 Camaro Z-28 equipment & options

Engine: Net horsepower down to 255 from 275 in 1971. Torque dropped 20 ft./lb. Flex fan replaced viscous drive. Chrome tailpipe tips removed.

Other details: Revised grille. Rear deck spoiler and fast-ratio non-power steering made optional instead of standard. Spoiler COPO 9796 renumbered RPO D-80, and front air dam added to now optional D-80 spoiler.

Power steering now had straight 16:1 ratio and was revalved to give more road feel. Hood and deck striping became a delete option. Revised rear stabilizer bar and rear shock valving.

1973 Camaro Z-28 equipment & options

Engine: Net horsepower down by 10, to 245. Torque still 280. Hydraulic lifters replaced solid ones. Aluminum high-rise manifold eliminated. Rochester Quadrajet carburetor replaced Holley 4-barrel. A 17-quart cooling system replaced 15-quart used since 1970½.

Other details: Price of Z-28 package lowered to $502.05. Positraction standard; 4.10:1 axle dropped. Air conditioning became available this year as a Z-28 option for the first time.

1974 Camaro Z-28 equipment & options

Engine: Same as 1973, but HEI (high-energy ignition) introduced in mid-year.

Other details: New, big, 4-color hood and deck decals (RPO D-88) optional. Black-painted grille with bright argent outline. Power steering standard in all Z-28's, with same ratios as in 1971 but more road feel. Aluminum gearcases for all 4-speed transmissions. Z-28 temporarily discontinued after 1974 model year.

1977½ Camaro Z-28 equipment & options

Engine: Hydraulic-cam 350 delivered 185 bhp and 280 ft./lb. torque. Cast-iron crank, 2-bolt mains. Cam tim-

ing: 280 degrees intake, 288 exhaust, 58-degree overlap, 0.410 inch lift. No mufflers but twin pipes with catalytic converters and resonators. Rochester 4-barrel carb.

Clutch: 11-inch diameter.

Transmission: 4-speed Borg-Warner T-10, aluminum case, Inland or Hurst shifter, 2.54:1 low (not available in California). Turbo Hydra-Matic 400 optional, mandatory in California.

Rear Axle: Ratios were 3.42 for Turbo Hydra-Matic and 3.73 for 4-speed; no options.

Brakes: Same as 1974.

Front suspension: The revived Z-28 became a handling package for 1977½ rather than a muscle package. Spring rates revised: 365 lb./in. instead of 300 previously. Stabilizer now 1.2 inch instead of 1.0.

Rear suspension: Springs 127 lb./in. for 1977 instead of 89-99 lb./in. for 1974. Rear stabilizer 0.55 instead of previous 0.69 inch. Higher durometer shackle rubber bushings with revised rear shackles. Revised shocks.

Steering: Power assist standard, ratio new straight 13.02:1 overall instead of 1974's 14.3:1.

Wheels & tires: 15 x 7 rims, Goodyear GR70-15 steel-belted radials standard.

Special equipment: Space-Savr spare standard. Specific decals on hood, front fenders, front and rear spoilers, wheel houses, rocker panels, and door-handle inserts.

1978 Camaro Z-28 equipment & options

Engine: Same as 1977½.

Other details: Identical to 1977½ in suspension and appointments.

1979 Camaro Z-28 equipment & options

Engine: Basically unchanged, but due to revised exhaust, carburetion, and ignition timing, horsepower dropped to 175 for 49-States versions and 170 bhp in California. Torque was also slightly lower this year.

Other details: Z-28 graphics changed for 1979, and instrument cluster revised along with other '79 Camaros.

Camaro Goes Racing

Chapter Seven

CAMAROS WON 18 OUT OF 25 Trans-Am races in 1968-69 and took the SCCA championship both years.

The Z-28's brief, hectic racing career peaked early, but it stands even today as a case study in the efficacy of science and technology. Computers helped create the first Camaro, and computers also helped it win races.

Not that Chevrolet Research & Development (R&D) deserves all the credit. Yet there's no doubt that the world's largest automaker, with the world's most sophisticated electronic equipment and the best brains in the business, did help Roger Penske and Mark Donohue get where they got in Trans-Am sedan racing.

Never mind the AMA racing ban of 1957, because that had a limited effect on most car manufacturers. Ford didn't observe it at all and said so. Chevrolet tightened and loosened its observance from year to year, sometimes sitting out whole seasons, sometimes participating quite directly.

During the period we're talking about—the late 1960's—GM's internal policy stated simply: *Thou Shalt Not Race.* However, the divisions got around this in various ways. Chevrolet didn't participate *directly* in racing, but it did lend a hand to competitors it felt could win. It helped them not so much with money (that, too, was indirect) but mostly with brains, research and test facilities, and by cataloguing special racing parts as needed. Giving these parts service numbers, cataloguing them and having them readily available made them legal for racing.

What did Chevrolet get in return? Favorable publicity, for one thing, and publicity was probably the most important overall benefit. By beating Mustangs on the race

After problems with SCCA in Oct. 1967, Smokey Yunick (in hat) decided to run his Z-28 at Bonneville. The car captured 259 world speed records in Classes B, C, and Unlimited. Yunick got Mickey Thompson, Bunkie Blackburn, and Curtis Turner to drive for him. With the 302 V-8, Yunick's Z-28 topped 174 mph, and with a 396 installed later, the same car did better than 183.

course, the Camaro was establishing itself as a performer and not just a Chevrolet copy of a Ford original.

The other benefit to Chevrolet came in terms of technical knowledge. As long as Chevrolet could learn from the Trans-Am effort, R&D would stay with it. Penske and Donohue were both trained engineers and could talk the same language as the Chevy engineering staffs.

Chevrolet at that time was just setting up computer models for cars of various types. Computer analysis and computer models were new then, and here was a chance for Chevrolet R&D to gather a storehouse of information and data to be used in engineering future production cars. By analyzing the problems and performance of racing cars, Chevrolet R&D could establish baselines for the ultimate vehicle performance then available.

Unlike the Corvette, whose baseline had relatively little application to bread-and-butter sedans, the Camaro's performance data could be used to help map out steering, braking, suspension, and other systems for production family cars.

Reports engineer Jim Musser: "We had already been through several years of race-car development with Jim Hall and, in fact, all the instrumentation and techniques had been established during the Chaparral days. These techniques were simply applied to the Camaro.

"I'd have to say that there was very little *new* knowledge added during the Camaro program. Rather, it was an application of knowledge already acquired as a result of the Chaparral program. It's true, however, when Roger Penske first started to work on the Camaros, he was working with . . . some of the product engineers who didn't have available to them the knowledge that had been acquired at Chevrolet R&D. However,

Dick Guldstrand, who'd set up Dana Chevrolet performance program after leaving Roger Penske, did well in 1967 West Coast events, won St. Jovite.

A Trans-Am Camaro, believed driven by Sam Posey, leads Cougar through a Riverside ess. Mustang team won the '67 SCCA series, with Cougar second.

when I moved into the product group as assistant chief engineer, we became involved with Penske's program, and we immediately applied the knowledge acquired by the R&D group.''

As an aside, Chevrolet R&D also studied the vehicle dynamics of other types of race cars; for instance dragsters. But they soon found that there was little to be learned. Drag racing involved only an engine developing lots of torque (which they already knew about) plus the effort of transmitting this torque to the ground (weight transfer, aerodynamics, and tire technology, essentially). So after studying dragsters for a few weeks, R&D moved back to road racing, which presented many more practical questions in terms of suspensions, brakes, transmissions, axles, tire dynamics, steering and braking controls, and so forth—much more interesting and applicable to everyday cars than any other type of racing.

Thus it became the good fortune of Penske Racing, Inc., to come in on the ground floor of Chevrolet's willingness to help potential Trans-Am winners. Roger Penske already knew a lot of people at GM and Chevrolet: Ed Cole, Frank Winchell, Bill Mitchell, John DeLorean, Bunkie Knudsen, Pete Estes, etc. Penske enjoyed a golden reputation as a man who could combine racing with salesmanship and engineering—a businessman whose enthusiasm ran to race cars. Jim Hall and his Chaparral racing team fit into the same general category. Hall, though, didn't care that much about Camaros, and Penske did.

To step back a moment—even before Penske got started campaigning Camaros, Dana Chevrolet in Los Angeles put together an early and quite successful 2-car team of Z-28's. Dana had taken delivery of five Z's in late 1966 and, under the direction of former Penske engineer/driver Dick Guldstrand, reworked four for SCCA competition. Two went to Ron Tonkin in Portland and two stayed at Dana. Guldstrand drove one of these Dana cars to victory in the 1967 St. Jovite race in Canada, thus giving the Camaro its first-ever Trans-Am win. He also did quite well in West Coast activities, winning Riverside and the Stardust race in Las Vegas before Penske got the nod.

R OGER PENSKE OWNED A STRING of Chevrolet agencies in Pennsylvania and New Jersey. He'd been an amateur racer in college, and he initially met Mark Donohue when both ran Formula Juniors.

According to former Chevrolet R&D engineer Paul van Valkenburgh, from whom most of the information in this chapter comes*, Penske invited Donohue to race on his dealerships' team in 1966. Donohue at that time was driving for Ford, but he also took on Penske's Can-Am effort that year.

During a lull in their racing schedule in the winter of 1966, Penske and Donohue began talking about preparing a new Camaro to run against the Mustangs in the recently announced SCCA Trans-Am sedan series. The more they talked, the better the idea sounded, so in Jan. 1967 Penske sent down George Wintersteen, a wealthy Pennsylvania sportsman, to pick up a brand-new Camaro Z-28 at the factory. Wintersteen drove it back to Penske's shops in Reading, Pa.

Penske, who then counted only on Sunoco for sponsorship, decided to prepare the Z-28 for the Daytona 24-hour race on Feb. 5, 1967. He put mechanic Murph Mayberry and Donohue to work beefing up the Z-28.

Since Donohue had run a Mustang at Daytona the previous year, Penske assumed he (Donohue) knew what to do to the Camaro. In his autobiography, Mark Donohue describes how wrong Penske's assumption had been and how he had no idea what spring rates the Z-28 should have for Daytona.

Penske and the Chevrolet engineers were pressing him for figures, but Donohue hedged and finally went to a spring shop in Philadelphia and asked them to make up a set of 4-leaf rear springs to replace the Z-28's Mono-Plate singles. When the shop foreman asked Mark how thick to make the springs, Donohue held up two fingers and said simply, "Oh, about yea thick."

*Paul van Valkenburgh has written two excellent books on the topic of Chevrolet and racing: *Chevrolet-Racing? Fourteen Years of Raucous Silence* (Haessner Publishing Co.), and *The Unfair Advantage,* Mark Donohue's autobiography done in consultation with van Valkenburgh (Dodd, Mead & Co.).

For the car's front suspension, Mark checked a Triangle Spring catalogue and bought three or four different coil sizes that would fit. As it turned out, the Z-28's front suspension ended up with spring rates of 1200 lb./in. in front and 400 in back (normal for street driving would be about 300 and 90 respectively).

The car, of course, handled terribly, and worse than that it had no brakes. Fourteen laps into the Daytona race, the engine quit with a clogged carburetor. It was probably a lucky thing, considering the brakes.

NEXT UP WAS SEBRING. To quote Donohue from his autobiography: "We went back to the shops and re-prepared the car for Sebring, and at Sebring we just couldn't do anything! It was the *worst* handling thing I had ever driven. It was so bad it was beyond belief. It had the same springs we used at Daytona, because we didn't know any better—and it was just awful. Then the brake problems started to show up, and I crashed it and tore the nose off. I qualified way down, and got in the race, but the Fords all ran away from us. The brakes went and we struggled along to finish second after Jerry Titus [in a Mustang]. At least we survived."

Actually second at Sebring wasn't bad, all considered. Chevrolet Product Promotion Engineering, under Vince Piggins, continued to support the Penske team and sent along special parts, including rear axles, transmissions, and optional suspension pieces. But the car still had virtually no brakes and relatively poor handling. Engines were built (or more accurately race-prepared) by Traco in California, and at least *they* were strong—in the 420-bhp range. The car would run, but it all but refused to stop.

The third Trans-Am race of the 1967 season was a 4-hour go at Green Valley, Tex. Donohue said afterward that the car was so hard to drive that he had to fight it all the way. He was totally exhausted after four hours, and Dan Gurney won the race in a Mercury Cougar.

At this point, Donohue decided something had to be done about the brakes. Chevrolet engineer Gib Hufstader tried various fixes—sintered linings, automatic adjusters on the rear drums, ducts for forced-air cooling, cutaway backing plates. Nothing helped. Hufstader at that point began the project of adapting Corvette 11.75-inch discs to all four wheels of another Camaro—a project that later ended up becoming RPO JL-8 for the 1969 model.

Donohue took the Penske Trans-Am car to Bridgehampton for a week to experiment further with the normal Z-28 disc/drum brakes. He had no choice but to lick the problem, and he called for Chevrolet's assistance.

Chevrolet engineers Dick Rider and Vince Piggins showed up to help. Rider attached thermocouples and pressure sensors to every part of the brake system. These gave temperature readings that showed no excessive heat, but they did show excessive pedal pressures. Conclusion: no conclusion. Much later, though, a second analysis of the data showed that by reversing the brake lines to the master cylinder, the disc/drum system could be made to work fine. Reversing lines made the larger piston in the split master cylinder serve the front discs, not the rear drums as on the stock system. Engineer Don Cox, who later worked for Penske, made the discovery.

The Bridgehampton brake session was important because it marked the first time Chevrolet engineers actively participated in race-preparing a Camaro. Two races later, the blue Penske/Sunoco #6 *still* came in second at Lime Rock and then third at Mid-Ohio. Donohue was invited to bring his car to the GM Proving Grounds near Milford, Mich., because Chevrolet, it seems, was getting tired of losing races and wanted to evaluate Penske's Camaro under controlled conditions.

CHEVROLET RESEARCH & DEVELOPMENT owned perhaps more and better equipment, had access to more and better facilities, and employed more and better people than any auto organization in the world, a situation no different today than in 1967. Dick Rider again became Chevy R&D's liaison, and Donohue had brought mechanic Roy Gane with him to Milford.

They were given a small area in the Proving Grounds shops, and they also had access to "Black Lake," a perfectly smooth and flat 59-acre area of asphalt that got its name

The 1968 and '69 seasons became Camaro walkaways. Mark Donohue (left) piloted most of the winning cars, which Roger Penske (right) sponsored.

Donohue kept the number 6 throughout his Camaro Trans-Am experience. Chevrolet backed the Penske effort with parts, computers, and test facilities.

Chevrolet's famous R&D telemetry van monitored important aspects of Penske's machines via radio that picked up signals from sensors on cars' brakes, steering, tires, pedals, etc. Computers inside the van could let engineers pinpoint weaknesses in both cars and drivers so that each could be improved for better lap times.

With Chevy's aid, Donohue's crew worked out a speedy system that used vacuum to help swap brake pads. It took Ford six months to figure out the secret.

Donohue takes checkered flag at Pacific Raceway near Kent, Wash., winning at 87.6 mph. Another Camaro finished fourth. Mark had won two Trans-Am races just before Kent, and this became 1967's last go.

Penske cars sprouted monitors everywhere. Special wrench let all five lugs be turned at same time.

Fully competitive Chaffey College Camaro used the 4-wheel discs plus factory rear stabilizer bar; also horizontal shock to help control axle judder.

by being indistinguishable from a lake when it rained. Ducks commonly try to land on it. Black Lake does have a 2-degree slope for drainage. A driver can slew around on it indefinitely without worrying about hitting anything or turning his car over. Pylons can be set up to outline courses of various shapes and sizes.

At Black Lake this first time out, the R&D people put sensors on the car to check such things as braking forces, aerodynamic drag, lift, and downforce; also camber change during cornering. Sensors were put on the suspension, body, and brakes, with radio transmission to a trailer full of computers that gathered and processed the information. At this early stage, Chevrolet R&D lacked experience in analyzing race cars, and they ended up with a lot of numbers they didn't yet know what to do with. But several lights did begin to click on from this session, notably that the Z-28's anti-windup bar on the right rear axle conflicted with suspension geometry and actually hurt handling. Also that the Camaro's unit body needed beefing up so it didn't itself become a suspension member. Later a welded-in rollcage gave the needed extra stiffness.

At the time the rollcage was going in, Penske learned about Mustangs lightening their bodies by acid dipping. In response, Chevrolet wanted to run off a special set of thin-gauge body panels for the Penske Camaro. This light sheetmetal was to be introduced into the standard Fisher body presses—an expensive proposition that Fisher rejected because it could permanently damage the Camaro's body dies.

T HE CAMARO'S 1967 LOSING STREAK lasted only one more race. At Bryar, in New Hampshire, an axle broke in practice and another let go in competition, forcing Donohue to crash.

But Piggins remedied the axle problem for the next go by increasing axle diameter and insisting on magnafluxing all parts before shipment. And Penske started using the same acid dipper who served the Mustang teams.

Chevrolet R&D was under Frank Winchell at the time, with Jim Musser his right-hand man. The race after Bryar was going to be Marlboro, Md. Musser knew about Donohue's continuing handling problems. The car still, despite hundreds of seat-of-the-

Jerry Titus' Mustang placed fourth in 1968 Daytona 24-hour race, besting all other ponycars. Mustangs and Camaros both used 4-wheel disc brakes.

pants fixes, had a tendency—as Donohue put it—to "leap and bound." It wouldn't cooperate in the corners and had to be power-slid through—not the fastest way to get around a race course.

Musser came down to Marlboro the weekend before the race, driving R&D's special tool van. This was a one ton Chevrolet truck outfitted with welders, compressors, power tools of every description, lifts, jacks, hoists, 110-volt generator, and parts galore. Among the parts for the Camaro were springs of every conceivable rate, with anti-roll bars to match.

While Musser did the thinking, Donohue and mechanic Roy Gane began swapping off suspension components, then trying the car on the track. It was the purest sort of trial and error and a total turn-around from the computer analyses tried at Black Lake. But it began to yield results.

After softening up the front springs considerably and likewise the rears, then adding a rear stabilizer, the Camaro finally began to handle. The chosen spring rates ended up being 550 lb./in. front and 180 rear.

Musser had gone to considerable trouble, too, to disguise the tool truck, even equipping it with Pennsylvania license plates. From the outside it could have been a vegetable van. There was no indication that Chevrolet had anything to do with it. After Musser left, a track guard said to Donohue: "Say, that engineer from Sun Oil—he's a pretty sharp, isn't he?"

Between shakedown runs at Marlboro and the race itself, Donohue and Gane took the Camaro back to Philadelphia and tore it down completely. They rebuilt everything: engine, transmission, brakes, and wiring. They went without sleep, living on sandwiches and taking an occasional shower under a garden hose. It now appeared, at long last, that the car was ready for competition.

AND IT WAS, because Marlboro became the first Trans-Am race the Penske Camaro won. Donohue and Craig Fisher shared the driving and finished ahead of Mustangs, Cougars, and Javelins at an average speed of 63.23 mph.

The Traco shops in California set up Penske's racing engines. Jim "Crabby" Travers (shown) and Frank Coon also built powerplants for competitors' cars.

Donohue dices with Parnelli Jones' Mustang at MIS. Parnelli eventually won, with Mark second. Mustang used the tunnel-port 302 with a 1200-cfm Holley.

Young lady helps her partner swap gears before AARC event in Bakersfield, 1969. Among the interesting touches are anti-roll bar and rear disc atop tire.

This win gave a great lift to the Penske and Chevrolet contingents, and Donohue finally felt good about the car. It handled as well as the best.

But a week or so later, as alternate Penske drivers Craig Fisher and Bob Johnson were trailering the Camaro westward toward California, tragedy struck. Their tow rigs went off a cliff near Reno and made junk out of everything—truck, trailer, and race car. Fortunately no one was hurt.

Penske had been working on a backup car, and he now airfreighted it out to Modesto, Calif., where qualifying for the next Trans-Am race was to be held the following day. They wired and painted the new car that night, then discovered they had the wrong axle gears.

Mark Donohue spent Saturday scouring Chevrolet dealerships in a 200-mile radius and finally found an axle with better gears. But they still weren't right, and the race went to Jerry Titus in a Mustang.

The last two races of the 1967 Trans-Am series—one on Oct. 1 at Stardust Raceway in Las Vegas and the final one near Kent, Wash., were both Camaro walkaways. The 3-mile road course at Vegas was considerably faster than the one at Marlboro, and Donohue managed to average just short of 95 mph for the race.

And at Pacific Raceway near Kent, his average speed was 87.6 mph. In that one, Donohue took the lead at the end of the first lap and never let go. Ron Bucknum's Mustang finished second, with Gurney's Cougar third and Bob Johnson in Penske's other Camaro (which had been rebuilt) fourth.

So the 1967 season hadn't been a complete washout despite getting off to a poor start and some bad luck along the way. The final points standing for 1967 put Mustang first, Cougar second, and Camaro third, with 68, 65 and 60 total points respectively. The 1968 season would prove considerably better.

IN WITH ALL THIS TRANS-AM activity, Smokey Yunick had also groomed a Z-28 for the final race of the season at Riverside, Calif. He'd built up a fantastically powerful engine and stretched various SCCA rules as had been the custom in NASCAR. The upshot was that SCCA at first wouldn't let Smokey run at Riverside.

Undaunted, Smokey trailered the car to Bonneville and ran it on the salt Oct. 19-26, 1967, taking a total of 259 Class B, Class C, and Unlimited world speed records. His drivers were Mickey Thompson, Curtis Turner, and Bunkie Blackburn, and all runs were made under USAC/FIA sanction.

In Class C for American stock cars with engines of 183 to 305 cid, Smokey's Z-28 flashed through the flying mile at 174.344 mph. This beat the previous record, set in 1963 by a Studebaker Hawk, by 27.2 mph. The standing 10 kilometers saw the Z-28 average 155.541 mph (versus 129.53 for the Hawk), at which time the Camaro's engine blew. Smokey fixed it, though, and afterward ran for 12 continuous hours at an official speed of 143-plus mph—some 40 mph better than the old record.

In the same car with an L-78 396 V-8—set up for Class B (305-488 cid) and Unlimited—Yunick's drivers ran even faster. The 396 topped out at 183.486 mph, upsetting the old flying five kilometer record (held by a 1962 Pontiac) by 30 mph. The 396 had set 28 Class B and Unlimited records for distances up to 75 miles by Oct. 23 when a burned-out ring and pinion ended the first attempt at a 12-hour run. Soon repaired, though, the car came back to take records up to and including the full 12 hours. For pure speed, the Yunick Camaro topped them all.

THE WINTER OF 1967 was filled with frenzied preparation, both at Chevrolet and in Penske's Pennsylvania shops. For the Trans-Am season to follow, Donohue built a 1968 Camaro based on knowledge gained in '67, with the 1967 Camaro readied as backup.

Chevrolet also built a racing Camaro, but not for racing. They wanted it to test various new innovations, like the 4-wheel disc brakes developed by Gib Hufstader and an independent rear suspension system assigned to Al Rasegan.

The independent rear axle came largely from the Corvette (as had the brakes), and it proved an uncomplicated installation. Yet in tests, the i.r.s. proved no better than a solid-axle Camaro. Paul Van Valkenburgh feels that enough experimentation with dif-

Donohue's front spoiler broke and dragged along the ground during race at Michigan International Speedway, so his pit crew frantically tore it off. Fuel derrick (left) plunged gasoline into huge filler in Camaro's decklid. Pictured at top, Mark Donohue leads Brad Dunn's Firebird in Michigan downpour.

ferent shocks and stabilizer bars might have improved it, but it wasn't worth pursuing, especially since as an option it would have been mighty expensive. Another little trick worked out on the R&D Camaro: vacuum-removable disc brake pads. Mustangs were coming into the pits in Trans-Am races, refueling, changing all four tires, and switching front disc-brake pads, all in about four minutes flat. Camaros, on the other hand, were having a tough time changing brake pads, and that slowed them down in the pits.

So engineer Bill Howell, working in Piggins' group, got busy on the problem and developed a system whereby engine vacuum held back the caliper pistons. The driver had a vacuum switch on the dashboard to control retraction. The pads could then be popped out "like bread out of a toaster" by the mechanic—and likewise in. That got the Camaros' pitstops down to about a minute and 40 seconds, and it took the Ford people about six months to figure out what Chevrolet was doing.

But one of the greatest innovations offered by Chevrolet was its so-called "telemetry van." This was another R&D truck—a Stepvan—but this time instead of being stuffed with tools and parts, it was chocked full of electronic gadgetry, computers, and radio-telephone equipment. It looked like something out of *Mission Impossible.* "The telemetry van had been in use for several years," notes Jim Musser, "in the Chaparral development program prior to the time it was employed on the Camaros."

The telemetry van soon let Chevrolet R&D monitor the most intimate details of a race car's performance, and also the performance of the driver. Instead of the rather narrow information that R&D had been getting in the past by hooking sensors to brakes, suspension, and body, the telemetry van now let them "see," in computer terms, nearly every motion and every reaction that took place just about anywhere in and on the car.

Transducers and sensors sent back information to the truck on such topics as vehicle speed, acceleration rate, cornering g-force, brake application and temperature, throttle position, and steering-wheel angle. The telemetry van could be parked at trackside or on the GM Proving Grounds as far as three miles away from the running race car, and inside it strip charts and computer readouts would come spewing out of the machines, all to be instantly read and analyzed or to be stored for future use.

The telemetry van also served a safety purpose, because often the Camaro would be miles away, at the far side of the race course. An accident would be instantly obvious to those inside the van.

Taking the van's purpose a step further, the information gleaned here could be incorporated into a computer model of a race car. At that point, R&D enginers could program a "car" they knew would perform in certain ways at given speeds. At higher speeds, it would "fly off the course." By introducing, say, different stabilizer bars or different spring rates or tires, they could now jack the computer model around so it wouldn't "fly off the course" at those speeds, thus saving untold hours of cut-and-try plus wear and tear on an actual car or driver.

When the computer model performed as the engineers wanted it to, they went out to their test Camaro and proved out the computer-suggested changes.

The same techniques that let R&D analyze and program a race car also let them analyze driving techniques. For example, Mark Donohue was found to get around certain sections of a track faster than Ron Bucknum (Ron was now driving for Penske). So by analyzing how Mark did it, Bucknum was able to lop a second or so off his lap time. Conversely, Ron could beat Mark through certain corners, and here Mark learned to improve *his* lap time. The clues came in reading steering-wheel angle, accelerator position, g-forces, etc.

THE 1968 TRANS-AM SERIES began again at Daytona, and this time the Penske team arrived very much readier than the year before. Even so, cracked heads and downtime in the pits put the Camaros second in class at Daytona—a disappointment although not a bad showing.

The Penske Camaros (there were now two running regularly) began to hit their stride at the next race—Sebring, a 12-hour enduro. Donohue qualified on the pole, with Smokey Yunick's now-legal car right beside him. Al Unser and Lloyd Ruby were driv-

Chaparral teammates Jim Hall (top) and Ed Leslie raced hard at Laguna Seca in 1970 but they hadn't had time to sort out suspension mods. At right, Tony DeLorenzo's Owens-Corning Camaro leads Paul Nichter's 1968 at Mid-Ohio. All four of these racing cars were running 302-cubic-inch powerhouses.

Marshall Robbins shows good style at 1971 Riverside Trans-Am. The flex ducts at each window aid interior cooling on this particularly hot day.

ing it. Behind them sat Jerry Titus in a Mustang and Craig Fisher in Penske's other Camaro.

Smokey's car, whose engine was still built for power and not durability, exploded early in the race, leaving the duel between Titus and the Camaros. There were many other cars—non-ponycars—entered, too, and in the end two Porsches came in 1-2. But to everyone's surprise and delight, the Penske Camaros finished 3-4, or first and second in GT class.

The crowd went wild. To think that a couple of American ponycars almost kept up with the hallowed Porsches! It marked the beginning of the Camaro's winning streak.

Without going into individual races, the Camaros continued to fare extremely well throughout 1968, ending the season with 10 out of 13 wins, including eight victories in a row. Whether to credit Chevrolet's computers or Penske's and Donohue's tenacity remains a moot point, but undoubtedly all worked together.

A couple of practical things did get learned in 1968. For example, Positraction sometimes did more harm than good, especially when the axle clutches engaged and disengaged rapidly. Donohue eventually got around this problem by tightening the clutches so much that, in effect, the Positraction rear end was totally locked at all times.

Another point: Tightening the bushings that hold the front stabilizer bar—as Donohue had done—is *not* an effective way to control body roll. Much better to simply install a heavier bar, assuming one is catalogued; and Chevrolet *had* released one.

F OR THE 1969 SEASON, Penske built up two entirely new cars and had a hard time getting their suspensions right. Even with help from GM's telemetry van and Black Lake skidpad, the 1969 cars at first didn't perform so well as the '68's had. Finally, Mark Donohue figured out that the front stabilizer bar hadn't been heat-treated properly and had caused continual changes in front-end preload. A replacement bar solved the problem.

Vendettas and petty feuds erupted between Penske and SCCA officials; also between

Mike Keyser's Porsche lifts a leg but Mo Carter's Camaro hangs flat. Keyser eventually won 1973 Camel GT; Carter came in fifth.

IROC races pit driver against driver in cars that are theoretically identical. Highly modified Camaros have been used every season since 1974-75.

Drafting at nearly 180 mph, Bobby Unser tucks his nose into A.J. Foyt's tail. Superstar Foyt won $137,000 and IROC championships in 1976-77.

IROC stages races primarily for TV. Camaros run 450-bhp Traco-built 350's that get 4.5 mpg. Bodies stand considerably lower than stock.

Tom Sneva tangles with Cale Yarborough's Camaro, both spin, and Tom does battle with guard rail. Despite minor bumps, both drivers walked away.

Tach and four gauges grace IROC Camaro interiors. Seats and pedals are adjusted to fit each driver—the principal difference between these cars.

For 1979, IROC Camaros take on latest Z-28 graphics and are cut down even lower than they were before. Second spoiler mounts on standard spoiler.

Penske and some other car owners and drivers. At one point Penske was ready to pull out of Trans-Am racing altogether, but another competitor's remarks made him so angry that he vowed vengeance by outrunning him.

Which eventually the 1969 Camaros did, and they again captured the season's championship, winning eight of the 12 races. But Penske's and Donohue's hearts had gone out of it, and Chevrolet wouldn't match the offer they got from American Motors for 1970. So Penske left Chevrolet as a racing partner and took on AMC.

By 1970, the bloom was coming off the competitive Camaros, and the new 1970½ body style for some reason didn't seem nearly so enticing to professional car builders and drivers.

On July 5, 1970, Milt Minter won at Donnybrooke (Minn.), averaging 96.67 mph. And at Watkins Glen, N.Y., Vic Elford finished ahead of even the very fast Penske Javelins but had to run 103.8 mph to do it. By 1971, Camaros were absent from the road-race winner's circles, and Chevrolet engineers were spending time on emissions and fuel mileage instead of race cars. The muscle era had passed.

WELL, NOT ENTIRELY, because Camaros came back into racing in 1974 in the IROC series. This is a terribly clever commercial venture created by Roger Penske, Les Richter, and Michael Phelps.

It's essentially a racing series tailored for television. The trackside audience is incidental when you consider that an estimated 9.36 million households watch each race on TV.

Four to five events are run a year, pitting superstar drivers from various types of auto racing against each other in *cars that are set up to be as similar as possible.* They're identical except for seats and pedals, which are tailored to each individual driver.

In other words, it's a race pitting driver against driver, not car against car.

The first IROC races in 1973 used Porsche Carrera RSR's, but Penske Racing, Inc., which sets up the identical cars, determined that it would cost about half as much to

prepare a set of identical Camaros and yet the action wouldn't slow down. So for IROC II in 1974-75, that's what he did.

All IROC Camaros since 1974-75 have been essentially identical. Fifteen are prepared each season—three for practice and 12 for racing. They use 350-cid Chevrolet V-8's with 12:1 compression, Edelbrock Scorpion manifold with Holley 4-barrel 850-cfm carb, Crane roller cam with solid lifters, Hedman tube headers, Shiefer clutch, a Weaver dry-sump oiling system, Borg-Warner T-10-X 4-speed transmission, 4-wheel Airheart disc brakes with 12-inch rotors, and fairly stock Z-28 suspension.

The engines put out about 450 bhp SAE net at 6500 rpm, with a 7000-rpm safe rev limit. For the Camaros' first three IROC seasons, Z-28 versions weren't available but they've been used since their re-introduction in 1977½, and the drivers feel the Z-28's do handle better.

Points as well as purses are given for winning and placing in each final race. As of 1977, A.J. Foyt had grabbed $137,500 in total IROC money and won season championships in 1976-77. Before that it was Bobby Unser who took the 1975 championship and who's accumulated nearly $100,000. Mark Donohue, who helped come up with specifications for the initial IROC Camaros, became the series' first champion in 1974, but driving Porsches.

Penske, then, is the man who sets up the cars, Les Richter, president of Riverside International Raceway in California, handles track arrangements around the country. And the third principal, Michael Phelps, is a Beverly Hills TV packaging agent who takes care of the television end of the operation.

Races don't usually last very long, because they have to fit into the timeframe of one-hour TV programming. Speeds easily approach 170 mph on the straights and usually average between 100 and 150 mph for the race.

Among the series' associate sponsors are Chevrolet, Goodyear, Bosch, Union Oil, Monroe shocks, and Citicorp. There's also a long list of accessory sponsors, including Traco Engineering, Stewart Warner, Hedman, Hurst, Aeroquip, Moon, etc.

Chevrolet people like to say that IROC stands for "Incomparable Race of Camaros."

Chapter Eight

Birth of the Second Generation

WILLIAM L. MITCHELL likes to say that the first-generation Camaro ended up being designed by committee, while the second became a designer's design. That statement might be an oversimplification, but it's basically accurate.

The first generation (1967-69) had to compromise its shape to some extent by sharing the 1968 Nova's cowl and front subframe. Not so the second generation, which became an all-new body, not compromised in any way. Yes, the Firebird shared the Camaro's basic structure, but these two cars evolved together this time, and they didn't conflict in purpose as did the first-generation F- and X-bodies.

In the 1970½ Camaro, the designer reigned supreme—a very different situation from the first F-Car's development, where engineers and policymakers called most of the important shots.

According to GM design vice president Irv Rybicki: "We started planning the second-generation Camaro and Firebird immediately after the first project ended. That second car, as I remember, wasn't developed in the studios *per se.* We initially sat down in what we call the body development room, where we package our vehicles, and we worked very closely with Jack Humbert and Dave Holls; we were in there with Vince Kaptur [a body engineer], and we worked every day to get the seat placed just right, the rockers where we wanted them, the cowl at a certain point, always with the mental picture of the silhouette we were after.

"We moved the elements around until we had the package that looked like it would present the kind of body shape we were after—a little shoulder on the car, the wheels right out with the skin, the proper height . . . ."

Irv Rybicki continues: "I always say to the creative staff in our building that if we can get the anatomy, the shape of the skin is easy. The key to the appearance of a car is in its structure, in its anatomy: where you place the seats, how high, how wide, its length, the correct tumblehome, the proper relationship of the wheels to the sheetmetal. If you've got those elements, you're going to get an automobile that's very appealing to the eye, and that's the way this one was."

ONCE THE ARCHITECTURE of the second-generation Camaro/Firebird was established, Chevrolet's Studio Three, under the direction of Hank Haga—and the Pontiac studio headed by Bill Porter—began their design studies concurrently. They developed the new body through the coordinated efforts of these two studios.

Responsibility for the second-generation Camaro's design was again Henry Haga's who, you'll remember, had also done the first go-round. Haga worked under the watchful eyes of corporate vice president Bill Mitchell and Chevrolet design executives Chuck Jordan, Irv Rybicki, and Dave Holls, all of whom were instrumental in the direction of the 1970½ body.

"The way the new car started out," remembers Dave Holls, "was with a high bone going through the fender crest, something like the first generation. We worked that over for quite a while and pretty hard. It was a soft car but with a high bone and a wide loop grille."

Irv Rybicki recalls the problems Chevrolet engineers were having in packaging the heater, air conditioner, radio, glove compartment, and instrumentation all within the limits of a lower cowl. "They were insisting to Hank Haga that we raise the cowl at least an inch. Hank brought this to my attention, so I met with the engineers, but they wouldn't budge. They wanted more space.

"Finally, realizing we were at a stalemate, I called in Bill Mitchell. Bill quickly resolved the situation in a meeting by telling the engineers that a low silhouette was critical to the sporty character of this car and that we absolutely weren't going to raise the cowl even a fraction of an inch."

The new shape didn't come easily at first, and a good 18 months passed before Haga's people determined the silhouette they really wanted—plus the front and rear ensembles.

Once they got on the right track, though, the entire car almost finished itself, and within six weeks the design was done.

"Yes, I agree that the second-generation F-body was much more a designer's car," writes Henry Haga from Germany. "It had the proportion, it had the dash-to-axle, it had the low cowl, and it had these things because it was specific and didn't have to share anything with any other vehicle."

Haga continues: "The first designs we worked on for the 1970½ Camaro—and this was back in 1966-67—carried the same simple loop grille that evolved from the 1969 Camaro. But Bill Mitchell wasn't content with such an easy solution. He wanted a front end that had a much fresher, more distinctive character.

"After many months of searching for a design, we chose the general direction of a vertical radiator flanked by sheetmetal catwalks between the fenders and hood. We also

Second-generation Camaro's initial styling direction picked up the 1969's recessed loop grille (above). Hank Haga's Camaro studio coordinated efforts with Bill Porter's Firebird designers from the outset (below) and evolved both coupes concurrently. William L. Mitchell rejected loop grille as too simple.

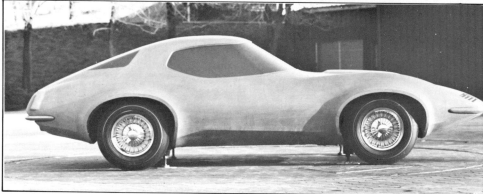

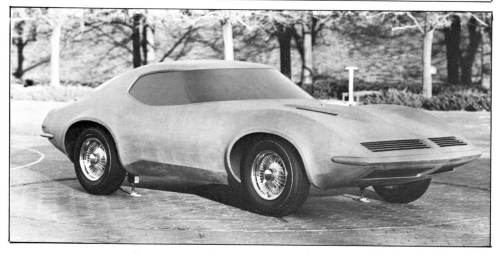

General shape of 1970½ Camaro began in mid-1966 with these 2-seater clay models. Haga's studio had responsibility for all Chevrolet small and sporty cars, so some of the Corvette's lines rubbed off on Camaro's second generation.

resolved an impasse between the low-cost front end and an alternate, more expensive proposal when we decided to make one the standard face and other, with its split bumper and urethane nose, the up-option Rally Sport version.''

WORKING IN THE CAMARO STUDIO with Haga were Jerry Palmer, Bill Molson, Jim Ferron, Jerry Brochstein, and Elia Russinoff. Jerry Palmer eventually became Haga's successor as studio chief. At the time, though, this team had responsibility for all Chevrolet small cars and sporty cars—the Camaro, Corvette, Corvair, Nova, and the upcoming Vega.

The Corvette's and Corvair's designs had largely stabilized after the 1968 models, so Haga's group divided most of its time between the 1970½ Camaro and the 1971 Vega. Originally, the redone Camaro was due to come out as a regular 1970 model, introduced in Sept. 1969 with other '70 Chevrolets. But complications of various sorts crept into the program, and introduction of the new body style had to be postponed until Feb. 1970—thus the 1970½ model designation.

The second-generation Camaro's silhouette came into focus before its front and rear aspects. One question that cropped up for a time was whether to include a rear quarter window. Many of the early clays did, but the eventual answer was simple. ''We saved $18 per car by eliminating that quarter window,'' states Dave Holls, ''and that paid for all the exotic underbody insulation, the extra carpeting, and we also got the longer doors out of it.''

Longer doors have better access to the rear-seat area, but some drivers later felt the doors were *too* long; too heavy to pull shut when parked parallel on a crowned street. The long doors also made (and still make) it hard to get out of the car in tight parking slots and narrow garages.

Another question about the body silhouette had to do with the height of the rear end. ''It's interesting to note,'' muses Henry Haga, ''that most of the designers and enthusiasts wanted to raise the tail of this car to give it a little more aggressive look. However, they were out-voted by some of the corporate leaders who firmly believed the rear end should terminate in a very slim horizontal loop.''

Early clays clearly showed the distinct rear loop, something like the 1968 Corvette's. The designers retained this and plugged in four round, Corvette-like (or Ferrari-like) tail lamps. The Camaro had a single-wall rear panel, while the Firebird, which again shared most elements of the revised F-body, took on a more expensive double rear panel, adding a flat insert behind the Camaro panel but keeping the Camaro tail as its inner trunk wall. If you look inside a Firebird trunk you can see the Camaro end panel.

TURNING NOW TO THE FACE of the 1970½ Camaro, Haga volunteers that, `` . . . the second-series Camaro front end was inspired very much by the Jaguar sedan front as it was first shown at one of the European autoshows.''

''We always talked about the Jaguar,'' confirms Dave Holls. ''Those secondary lamps in the catwalks were definitely Jaguar. But we also talked about the Facel Vega and the Aston Martin. Because of the relationship of all those cars—the fact that they're all expensive—instantly made the Camaro look like a more expensive car than the simple loop grille would have. The loop was just a mouth. A lot of cars have mouth grilles, but we wanted this one associated with very expensive cars.''

Two different upper designs evolved. Haga's studio developed an upper having the windshield wrap around the cockpit horizontally. Bill Porter's Pontiac studio designed the other—a windshield that formed a wide, open, upside-down U slanting back from the cowl.

Porter's concept was eventually selected, along with his side-window treatment, back light, and the softer, more fluid upper. His windshield pillars were shaped like the stems of stemware glasses—widening as they approached the roof. The windshield was initially modeled in a 60-degree slope, ``. . . which we all loved,'' remembers Porter, ''But it lost out to the current 57-degree windshield for cost reasons.''

The important eventuality, though, was that the U-shaped windshield as well as the rest of the F-body upper were released from a Pontiac studio.

By Oct. 1966, Kamm rear treatment made its appearance. Management liked it so much they insisted it be incorporated in later renditions. Wraparound rear glass also debuted but wasn't put into production until 1975. By July 1967, Camaro designers began to work with centered grille (top). Clays carried Chaparral nameplates.

Designers weren't sure what to do about rear quarter windows, so they tried several different roof treatments. The question was finally resolved when it

became clear that to eliminate the rear quarter panes and their roll-up mechanism would save $18 per car. This money later went to upgrade the interior.

Photos on these two pages show evolution of '70½ Camaro's rear and face. Jaguar sedan, Aston Martin influenced drawings and clays produced in early '68.

An interesting sidelight on the F-bodies—one that's not generally known—is the fact that second-generation Camaro and Firebird doors don't interchange. They never have. They're entirely different. The second-generation Camaro door has a sharp horizontal peak along its mid-line, while the Firebird door has a gently rounded section.

And with the doors being different, the rear fenders have to be, too. The Camaro's door ridge demands a corresponding ridge in the rear-quarter sheetmetal, whereas the Firebird's flank remains more rounded.

Although attempts were made to commonize Camaro and Firebird doors and rear fender sides, they're still separate and different even today. Designers in the Chevrolet and Pontiac studios have felt strongly down through the years that this subtle differentiation was valid and necessary. Their aesthetic feelings have won out against financial restraints, but since each car has to have its own set of door and rear-quarter dies, the expense of tooling additional body styles, such as a convertible or Kammback, would have doubled the total cost.

"There *was* a very slick-looking convertible mocked up on one clay model of the 1970½ Camaro," recalls Henry Haga. "But this proposal was shelved because of high tooling costs versus a relatively small number of projected sales."

Later, the Camaro studio also developed an interesting station wagon, or "Kammback," version of the second generation. The Kammback's rear side windows wrapped up into the roof. Since the Camaro and Firebird doors and rear fenders *were* different, the duplicate tooling needed for the Kammback meant that neither division got it. Tooling would simply have been prohibitive. If the Camaro and Firebird *had* shared doors, though, the Kammback F-body might well have gone into production.

The lack of common doors and rear fenders is only one example of how strong the designers' influence was on the second rendition of the F body. The styling groups weren't about to compromise their positions. Chevrolet and Pontiac wanted their individual versions to be as distinctive as possible.

One engineer later bemoaned the expense of the Camaro and Firebird going their own ways. "We'd initially told management that the two cars were going to share body com-

ponents. But it was a helluva job keeping them that way. A lot of insignificant differences crept in—door panels and other shapes that were different in such minor detail that the customer couldn't tell, yet we spent good tooling money from both divisions. It was kind of an uncontrolled program in that respect."

On an entirely different topic but one that has to be included before we leave the 1970½ Camaro's exterior styling: "Just before the second-generation 1970½ Camaro came out," reflects Hank Haga, "some people in the corporation got worried about the roundness of the car. This is a common phenomenon—it seems that whenever a really new car is about to be released, fear seizes some of those who've been working on it. Either they worry about their responsibility if the car doesn't sell or, perhaps more realistically, they worry because they really don't know the product.

"In any event, all anxiety was dispelled one day when Stirling Moss, the race driver, was given a sneak preview of the 1970½ Camaro. This was in the Design Center auditorium several months before announcement. He was ecstatic and, contrary to what some people felt, Moss was enthusiastic about the round, elliptical sections and related them to his feelings for a Grand Prix racing car."

AT THE SAME TIME Henry Haga's studio was wrestling with the 1970½ Camaro's exterior, George Angersbach's group, under Don Schwarz's direction, was hard at work on the evolution of the new body's interior. Schwarz by this time had been promoted to staff assistant and was in charge of all interior operations, with Angersbach responsible for all Chevrolet interior studios.

Back to Irv Rybicki: "A lot of time on the interior was spent on *human engineering*. We were aiming at something that was close to the Corvette in terms of ride and handling and ease of operation. This had to be a driver's car, with the shift lever correctly placed relative to the steering wheel; all the controls just right.

"For example, if you sit in a Camaro with your hands on the steering wheel, after the seat is properly adjusted, let your right hand drop off the wheel. It simply falls on the shift knob. The door latch is right where it should be. Every control is equally well plac-

ed. The interior is a very good job of human engineering. It's about as good a car in terms of human engineering as you'll find on the road today. Now I'm talking about the front seats, of course, not the rear.''

Turning to Don Schwarz, we come now to the creation of the 1970½ Camaro's instrument panel. ''That's the 1978 panel, too—it hasn't changed much in all these years.

''Honestly, we had a terrible time with the instrument panel on that car. I'd been promoted, and George Angersbach got the Chevrolet Interiors job. The studio had been struggling to come up with a design, and they just hadn't gotten anything fresh.

''But one evening I walked into the studio, and George had sketched out this panel design on a little 3 x 5 card. He showed me the concept, and it looked good to me. I said, 'If you feel that's what you want, then do it.' That was the cluster with the crook in plan view and the thin right side that rolled over. George did the rough sketch, and the next day the studio got to work on it, modeling the thing up, and from there it went real quick.''

When we asked George Angersbach for his recollections of the second-generation's interior design, he told us:

''We tried to give the Camaro an image that was specific to that vehicle, so we said, 'Okay, generally it has the character of the Corvette, but it's really more like comparing a sports-racing car to a rally car.' So we said the Camaro should have the features the driver would enjoy, and we grouped the instruments around the steering column. We grouped the controls close to the instruments and close to the steering wheel. As you know, we got the light and wiper switches located as close to fingertip control as we could.

''And out of this evolved this shrouded look. It gave us a very simple kind of instrument panel lower, which then would house the air conditioning controls and the heater and radio. And we thought that was a very sporty kind of look.''

What about the difficulty in arriving at the final design, we asked Angersbach. We heard that it took some hard work.

''It did,'' George replied, ''because it required an entirely different instrument panel construction. We went to plastic, for one thing, and because of the switch of materials and the emphasis for doing something different from the Firebird—I think this meant

quite a challenge for Chevrolet and one that didn't come easily in the early stages.

''We started out, for instance, with a console that went all the way into the rear seat area, just as it had on the Super Nova showcar way back when. The console joined up with the instrument panel right in the radio area. So it had the flavor of the Corvette without really borrowing any of the Corvette's appearance. In fact, this console design went so far that it was costed out that way.''

What about the 3 x 5 card that Schwarz had mentioned?

''That design proposal on the 3 x 5 card,'' answered Angersbach, ''was actually a cleaned-up version of a quick sketch we'd initially done on a wet napkin. The napkin had been doused with spilled coffee as the result of a frenzied design session . . . .

''The original concept had a shelf-like pod on the steering column. This pod carried the switches for lights, wipers, and turn signals. So it included a lot of things that never made it into production. But it did have that shape—the double-bent shape. It didn't stray too much from that. And we kept the passenger area very simple so that all the concentration of interest was in front of the driver.''

Another innovation inside the 1970½ Camaro was its seat construction. These were full foam buckets, with no metal springs of any sort. They were comfortable, with low backs and adjustable headrests that allowed good rear vision. The 1970½ seats contained 85% fewer parts than the previous year's Camaro buckets.

Fisher Body Div. developed the all-foam seats, and they were shared by the Firebird. Today, many GM cars use full foam seats, but these were the first. In 1971, the all-foam bucket seats were replaced in the Camaro and Firebird by modified versions of the high-back Vega seats.

WE TURN NOW TO THE ENGINEERING side of the 1970½ Camaro and find that most of the basic 1967-69 concepts were carried over into the new body style: the subframe, the unitized main section, most engines were the same, and the 11-inch front disc brakes—now standard— were those that had previously been optional on the Camaro. The 9.5-inch rear drums were carried over intact. So mechanically, the new car came along as evolutionary, not revolutionary.

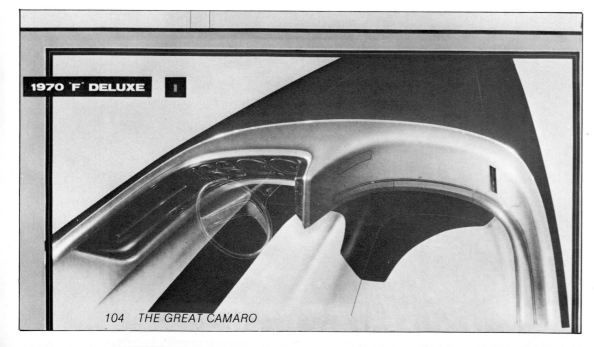

1970 'F' DELUXE

104   THE GREAT CAMARO

The new car would use plastics more extensively than before, so designers could deal in wilder visions—like the split theme at left. Clay above reveals early controls grouped around steering column. George Angersbach, working under Don Schwarz, initially sketched double-bent panel on a napkin. Camaro's front compartment layout tried to stress human engineering and driver convenience.

(Right) *By mid-1968, the '70½'s design needed only detailing. Note the two windshield treatments—Haga's wraparound with thin, dark pillars versus Porter's inverted U-shaped glass with stemware pillars.*

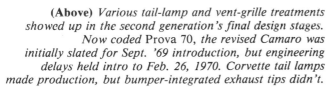

(Above) *Various tail-lamp and vent-grille treatments showed up in the second generation's final design stages. Now coded Prova 70, the revised Camaro was initially slated for Sept. '69 introduction, but engineering delays held intro to Feb. 26, 1970. Corvette tail lamps made production, but bumper-integrated exhaust tips didn't.*

But there *were* definite differences in terms of engineering refinement. The front suspension, while of the same type as before, didn't interchange with its predecessor; in fact no piece of it did.

Steering linkage was entirely different, too, and contributed to the new car's better handling. Gone forever were the single-leaf rear springs, and Camaros with the Z-28 and F-41 options from 1970½ on used anti-roll bars both front and rear.

The body became much more rigid and better insulated—a real *tour de force* among unitized bodies. It got rid of interior gaps and holes through which noises might otherwise have sifted in, and the double roof panel represented a major step forward.

Wheelbase remained identical, yet the rear compartment shrank, and so did the trunk. Now, instead of 8.3 cubic feet of usable luggage capacity, the 1970½ Camaro had only 7.3. Instead of 54.6 inches of effective hip room in the rear seat, the new F-body gave only 47.3 inches. But no matter, because the coupe was becoming even more a *gran turismo* or 2 + 2 and buyers realized that the rear compartment was meant for children or occasional seating only; also that on long trips you either traveled light or bought a trunk rack.

Alex Mair, Chevrolet's chief engineer from Aug. 1966 through Sept. 1972, recalls the beginning of engineering development of the 1970½ F-Car, when it became the engineers' chore to package the drivetrain in space requirements allotted by the designers. To quote Mr. Mair:

"Henry Haga is one of those designers who, when you came into his studio, had you excited about what he had to show. But sometimes he had design ideas that we felt were quite impractical to produce. This car's cowl was designed so low that we kept getting after Henry to be more practical and raise it up to the point where we could get aircleaners and engines under it.

"But his insistence kept the car low, which turned out to be a good thing. The engineers had to design new aircleaners, manifolds, and carburetors for the car, and we did manage to get everything under the hood. It's turned out to be an automobile that's been so attractive that, with only moderate changes over the course of nine years now, we still have more people wanting Camaros and Firebirds than we can build."

Body engineer Jack Hakspacher adds, "We modified the front subframe slightly in order to lower the car. The second-generation Camaro was considerably lower than the first. It presented a little tougher design job because we had to package basically the same elements in a smaller environment."

TO HELP LOWER THE CAR, the 1970½ subframe splayed outward toward the rear and was made wider so it attached nearer the rocker sills. These rockers, by the way, still had the wash-and-dry cleaning and ventilation action of the previous design. The idea again was to keep down corrosion.

The entire 1970½ front end, including suspension and brakes, took on modifications that later ended up being adopted by all of General Motors' 1975-78 X-Cars (the Nova family, which included Ventura, Omega, and Skylark) and the 1973-77 A-Cars (Chevelle, LeMans, Century, and Cutlass). Paul van Valkenburgh, in his book about Chevrolet in racing, feels that the second-generation Camaro front suspension evolved from experience gained by studying race cars (see Chapter Seven).

The 1967-69 Camaros had had their steering linkage *behind* the axle centerline—not a *bad* system but one that contributed to excessive steering angle under hard cornering and produced mild oversteer. By moving the steering linkage *ahead* of the axle for 1970½, steering deflection during cornering ended up contributing not to oversteer but to understeer, which tends to be a stabilizing condition in the hands of the average driver. The second generation's steering linkage, then, became altogether different, and there were other suspension modifications as well.

Alex Mair elaborates: "One of the purposes in getting the 1970½ F-Car into production was to introduce a new corporate front suspension in that car, and it's still used today. It has the disc brakes standard, and it had front-steer—the tie rods ahead of the suspension. It also had a nodular cast-iron steering knuckle.

"Those were features of a suspension that Charlie Rubly was heading up doing, open

to the whole corporation, and the suspensions from there forward were all developed *from* that car. So that was another reason for getting the redesigned F-Car going.

"One idea in choosing the revised F-Car to pioneer that front suspension was that it's always been perceived as a super-handling car. So all the effort put into it was to make a suspension that had great charcteristics for control and then hand it down to the other car lines.

"The F-Car proved to be such a good vehicle that subsequently, in 1975, we took those suspension parts and modified the X-Car to take the same components. So the 1975-78 X-Car had that suspension under it—even the same subframe."

BUT THE BIGGEST CHANGE of all came in the new F-Car's body— and not just in its appearance but especially in its engineering. For that story, we turn to engineer Chuck Hughes, whose group at the GM Proving Grounds tested the early second-generation component cars and suggested improvements as the program went along.

"Our component cars were cobbled up from 1969 Camaros, with handmade versions of the new subframe and suspension under them. This had the steering linkage, of course, ahead of the axle. Our technology told us that the new linkage would give us deflection understeer, and it did. Also, the frame rails were spread wider apart and went out nearer the rockers. So the 1969 underbody was altered for use as the 1970½ component cars.

"More important, though," continues Hughes, "was the activity of this body development group that we'd put together out at the Proving Grounds. We operated a sort of advanced 'how-to-make-a-body-better' group under Bob Robinson. Bob had several experienced people under him, and what they were interested in developing was better body *seals.* They were welding up the insides of cars.

"Generally, what we wanted to do was to have a car that, if you took the inside trim out of it and looked at the sheetmetal, wouldn't be full of holes. It would be solid, so you could put just a little trim over it, and with just a bit of panel padding you'd have a car that was quiet and simple to build.

"We had people spending a tremendous amount of time with the Fisher design engineers getting that put together, particularly in the sail-panel and package-shelf areas of the back seat where so many trim junctions mate with sheetmetal junctions and you have holes for noise to come in.

"Everyone went to a lot of trouble determining how to fold the metal at the top of the sail panel so it doesn't pipe noise from the trunk up into the headliner and then dump it out into the car. This came in the welding—it's a body that welds together solid. Working out the welds wasn't easy, because you do need welding access holes to build these cars, but we were able to move them. We tried to keep them away from cracks and corners. It took attention to detail.

"When we started out trying to plug up the holes, we didn't understand how to do it. It was a fairly 3-dimensional thing, and we had a lot of show-and-tell's where we used little colored wires, routing them through holes and cracks and crannies and running them around inside the body to show how noise paths happened and how junction seals happened. It was like a jigsaw puzzle.

"Another thing that came out of it is the double-panel roof, with the accoustical headliner and the padding sandwiched in between.

"And you know, we've had this body a long time now. It's been an extremely durable package. It's never had a seam that's loosened up after being beat on a rough road. It stays together well. And I just have to give an awful lot of credit to Fisher's cooperation on it and their putting up with us and Bob Robinson's body development group.

"The F-Car body was developed before we had good structural analysis groups to bring facts out. We would spend time over at Fisher asking, 'Can you turn this flange another way?' and they'd say, 'Of course, no problem at all.' In the early design stages they could do those things quite easily.

"It's my impression that that's probably the best inherently sealed rear passenger compartment of any car that's been put together."

Station-wagon versions of both Camaro and Firebird would probably have been produced if basic coupe doors and rear-fender panels had interchanged. Firebird Type K wagon (right) highlighted many autoshows here and abroad.

Chapter Nine

Camaro—the Timeless Machine

WHO COULD HAVE PREDICTED such an unusually long life for the second-generation Camaro and Firebird?

Some forecasters, in fact, said just the opposite. In its May 1970 issue, CAR & DRIVER prophesied that the restyled, re-engineered F-body would soon wither and die from lack of sales. The second-generation Firebird and Camaro, said the magazine, would end up costing General Motors millions of dollars due to a monumental miscalculation of the ponycar market.

The case could certainly be made. In 1967, ponycars had captured 13% of total U.S. new-car sales. By 1969, that figure had dipped to 9.2%, then 3.4% in 1972. The decline of the muscle car, rising insurance rates, a 6-month UAW strike in 1972, the Vietnam war, and then the Arab oil embargo of Dec. 1973 all contributed to a softening of the ponycar market.

By 1975, all ponycars except the Camaro and Firebird had either been deep-sixed or drastically resized. The Mustang grew smaller, the Cougar larger, and the Bar-

racuda, Challenger, and Javelin went the way of the Edsel.

Even the Camaro and Firebird entered the list of endangered species. General Motors' top management seriously considered dropping both cars in 1972. Only concerted lobbying by a hardcore group of Chevrolet and Pontiac executives saved the F-Car.

And partly *because* the Camaro and Firebird kept to their original ponycar size and concept—and *because* they perservered while all competitors left the

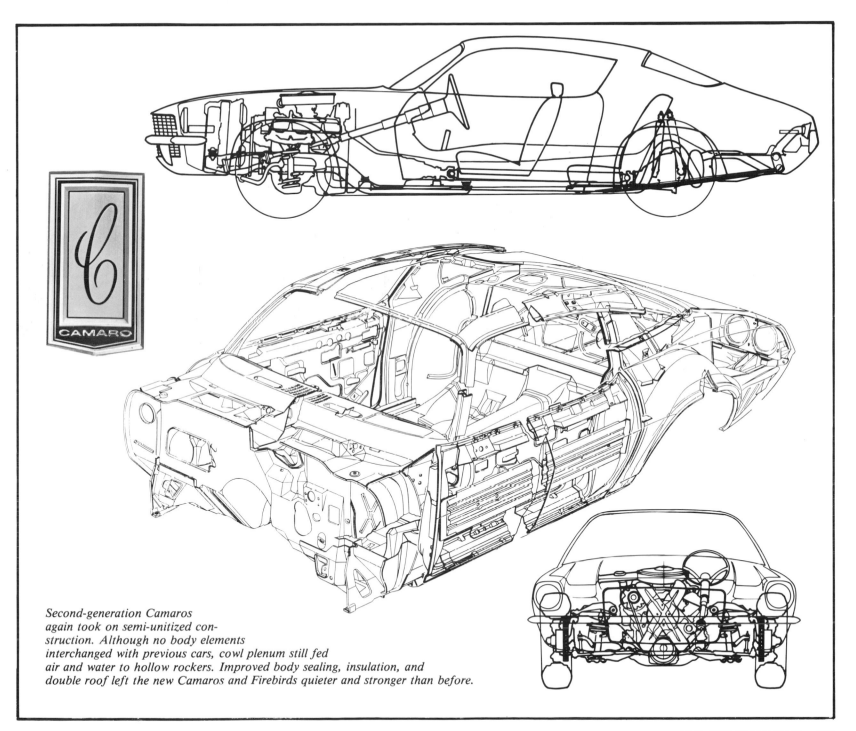

Second-generation Camaros
again took on semi-unitized construction. Although no body elements
interchanged with previous cars, cowl plenum still fed
air and water to hollow rockers. Improved body sealing, insulation, and
double roof left the new Camaros and Firebirds quieter and stronger than before.

Camaro designers had modeled a 1970½ convertible, but the closest they came to building one was this special landau showcar for entertainer Glen Campbell.

Design vice president William L. Mitchell's personalized 1970½ Camaro carried ZL-1 Berlinetta nametags, ran the Corvette aluminum-block 427. Modified in 1972, it led to slope-grille design introduced for 1974.

field—have these two automobiles staged such an unprecedented comeback. They now dominate the traditional ponycar field and have no direct competition.

Camaro sales tripled between 1972 and 1978. Firebirds have fared similarly well. It's a phenomenon no one could have foreseen in the first half of this decade, least of all in those dark, gloomy days following the energy crisis.

General Motors has stayed with the second-generation F-Car perhaps longer than any other body in its history. Except for minor cosmetic changes, it's still basically the same car today as in 1970½. GM insiders say the Camaro and Firebird will keep this body at least through the 1981 model year. After that, the F-Car might be downsized and could end up with front-wheel drive and V-6 turbo power.

The 1970½ Camaros

ROAD & TRACK called the 1970½ Camaro the "first serious effort since the 1963 Corvette to create a real American GT."

As mentioned, the second-generation Camaros entered dealer showrooms on Feb. 26, 1970, as midyear offerings. The 1970½ Corvette and Firebird debuted at the same time.

The Camaro for 1970½ came as a 2 + 2 coupe only—no more convertible. It spanned the same 108-inch wheelbase as before, but nary a body panel nor suspension member interchanged with the previous generation.

The new Camaro stood two inches longer, 0.4 inch

Rally Sport group included hidden wipers, bright moldings above windows, double tail-lamp bezels. Turbine wheelcovers from Corvette were optional.

Revised subframe splayed out more and stretched farther rearward, as shown in Chevrolet lobby display.

Split bumper, Endura grille identified Rally Sport.

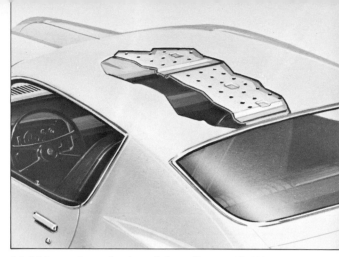

Multi-layered roof, shared by all post-1970½ Camaros, absorbed 56% more sound than before.

Easiest way to tell 1970½ Camaro from 1971-73 is by low-back front seats. Foam-filled buckets shared some structural elements with earlier models. Wide doors gave better entry and exit to rear compartment.

Stirrup shifter carried over, as did standard steering wheel, but with modified center section.

wider, and 1.1 inch lower than before. Front and rear tread were wider by 1.7 and 0.5 inches respectively. Glass area, despite the lack of rear quarter windows, increased by nearly 10%. And doors were five inches longer than previously.

Chevrolet carried over most of the Camaro's engines and drivetrain components from 1969, but with a few important exceptions. Gone were the 302 and 325-bhp 396 V-8's; also the 230-cid 6. The previous year's optional 250-cid 6 became standard.

A 454-cid, 450-bhp, high-performance V-8 with 3 x 2 carburetion and aluminum heads was initially slated for the 1970½ Camaro but apparently never made it. Chevrolet's early specification sheets all listed this LS-7 454, so we decided to include it in our specs as well. There's no record, however, that any of these large engines was ever installed in a Camaro at the factory.

The Camaro LS-6 454 V-8 was a 1970 derivative of previous Chevrolet 427 V-8's. The 1970½ Corvette listed two 454's—an LS-5 and an LS-6—at 390 and 460 bhp respectively.

Actually, the 1970½ engine/transmission situation for Camaros turned out to be even more confusing than that. The 396 V-8, for example, no longer really displaced 396 cubic inches. For reasons unexplained, Chevrolet chose to increase this engine's bore from 4.094 to 4.126 inches in 1970½. This gave the ''396'' an actual displacement of 402.2 cid. No one knows why this happened nor why Chevrolet didn't call the 402 a 402 instead of a 396.

The base 307 V-8 no longer came with a 4-speed option. Instead, you could get the 307 with a Chevrolet-built manual 3-speed or optional Powerglide or Turbo

Chevrolet originally intended to include the 454 V-8 in the 1970½ Camaro's lineup but cancelled at the last moment. Standard V-8 remained 200-bhp 307 (left), augmented by 350's and 402-cid "396" engines.

In 1971, Camaros began using modified Vega front seats, with high backs and integrated headrests. Optional seat mechanism (AN-6, not shown) gave 4-degree tilt. NK-4 wheel (shown) went standard in '73.

Hydra-Matic. The heavy-duty 3-speed and Torque-Drive were discontinued.

All 350 and larger 1970½ V-8's mated to 4-speeds as their standard transmissions, with Turbo Hydro optional on all but the L-78 396. All 1970½ V-8's, incidentally, got new cable-type accelerator linkages plus heavier anti-lift engine mounts. And the L-48 350's revised, deep-cover fuel pump incorporated the vapor return line.

Camaros carried over all major options and option groups for 1970½, including the Style Trim package, Rally Sport, Super Sport, and Z-28. In addition, there was again a Special and a Custom interior.

To recognize these various packages and combinations, here's a brief rundown on their major differences.

The basic, plain-Jane 1970½ Camaro came with small, baby-Moon-like hubcaps, exposed flat-black wipers, bright single bezels around all four rear lamps, and the straight-across bumper. It also carried a wide chrome rocker molding and, if the car had one of the 350-cid V-8's, it showed engine identification plates on both front fenders. With any other engines, it didn't.

The Style Trim group (Z-21; $52.70) added bright moldings for the roof gutter, rear edge of the hood, and an additional ring around each of the four rear lamps. It also had color-matched door handles.

Next up came the Rally Sport, with its free-standing grille and twin bumperettes (Z-22; $168.55). The RS incorporated everything in the Style Trim group plus adding the split bumper, color-matched urethane grille frame with rubber central strip, parking lamps on the catwalk between the headlights and grille, hidden wipers, and RS fender identification. The RS option could be combined, as before, with either the Super Sport or Z-28 package.

In the Super Sport option (Z-27; $289.65), the L-48 350 came standard, or you could order the L-34 or L-78 396's with 4-speed. Turbo Hydra-Matic was optional for the L-48 and L-34. The SS-396's came with black-painted trunk panels. The rest of the SS package consisted of a special black grille, hidden wipers, power brakes, bright engine trim, special hood insulation, 14 x 7-inch wheels with F 70-14 bias-belted white-letter tires, chromed dual exhaust tips, and SS identification inside and out. You also automatically got the F-41 suspension with the 396's because those V-8's weighed 180 pounds more than the 350.

We've talked about the Z-28 and what it entailed (see Chapter Six), but keep in mind that most buyers did combine the Z with the Rally Sport. Remember, too, that all 1970½-72 Camaros with the split front bumper had catwalk parking lamps, while cars with the straight-across bumper placed the parking lamps underneath the blades in the bumper pan.

That year's Camaro listed 15 exterior colors, five interior colors, and three hues of vinyl tops: black, white, or dark green.

Steel-backed Endura molding surrounded 1970½-73 RS grille. Rally wheels cost $45.30. Sport mirrors came with SS and Z-28 but not with Rally Sport.

Interiors now came with bucket seats only—no more optional bench since 1968. All-vinyl interior colors were black, bright blue, dark green, saddle brown, and sandalwood. Doors and sidewalls were trimmed in matching vinyl panels, and carpeting was standard.

One step above the base 1970½ interior came the Special interior group (Z-23; $21.10), also called the Accent group, which included woodgrain appliques on the instrument cluster, steering wheel, and instrument panel, carpeting on the lower doors, a glovebox light, added body insulation, and a trunk mat. In addition to the standard five interior colors, the Custom interior offered a choice of expanded vinyl and fabric seat inserts in four additional 2-tone combinations.

The only gauges in the base instrument panel were for fuel and speed. You had to buy RPO U-14, the special instrument cluster, to get working gauges, tach, and clock. It was a mandatory option with the Z-28 and cost $84.30 extra. All instruments now mounted in the main panel, not on the console as before. The console, incidentally, was again optional (D-55; $59) and included woodgrain accents when ordered with the Custom interior.

Side guard beams inside the doors constituted a safety improvement. And as mentioned in Chapter Eight, the new body structure was engineered to minimize holes where noise might enter. A totally different approach to

When Camaro and Firebird assembly lines in Norwood, Ohio, ground to halt for the 174-day UAW strike of 1972, some 1100 cars were simply abandoned in various stages of construction. These two photos show the deserted lines.

All partially assembled 1972 Camaros and Firebirds had to be scrapped because they couldn't meet '73 bumper laws. GM estimated its dealers lost $125 million, and union losses came to $25 million in wages and benefits.

acoustics also helped. Fisher developed new sealing techniques for panel joints, new lip seals for the side windows, and new adhesives for bonding the windshield and backlight into their frames.

But the greatest acoustical advance came in the 1970½ Camaro's double roof. Here, the sound-absorbing system consisted of a laminate made up of the perforated headliner, a thin Mylar Tuflex blanket, then a perforated sheetmetal inner roof separated by a slight air gap from the normal outer steel top. In all, this roof system absorbed 84% of the resonance present inside the car—as opposed to 28% for the 1969 Camaro roof.

Better sound insulation also came about via a new one-piece dash mat; thicker foam-rubber seals at the firewall, hood, and cowl; the steel luggage-compartment barrier; and the stressed floorpan that was engineered for less resonance. As time went on, the Camaro's acoustical technology would advance even more.

The 1971 Camaros

You'd be hard pressed to distinguish a 1971 Camaro from the 1970½ because there was virtually no external change. The easiest way to tell one from the other is by the '71's high-back seats.

These had tall, integral headrests, while the 1970½ models were the only Camaros with full-foam, low-back seats and separate headrests. These 1971 seats were adapted from the Vega, using Vega seat frames with Camaro upholstery. An optional 2-position lever (AN-6; $19) allowed the driver's seatback to be adjusted through four degrees of tilt.

Otherwise, the 1971 Camaro got some new optional wheelcovers, 12 new paint colors, revised interiors, thinner windshield glass, two more colors added to the vinyl top selection, and a front air dam added to the optional D-80 spoiler. The low spoiler was still standard equipment for the Z-28.

Under the hood, all engines ended up lower in horsepower due to GM's across-the-board decrease in compression ratios. This decrease was mandated by General Motors management to accommodate unleaded and low-lead fuels.

The L-34 and L-78 396 V-8's (350 and 375 bhp) were deleted and replaced by a single 396, the LS-3, rated at 300 bhp. A 400-cid V-8 appears to have been planned for midyear introduction but never materialized in the Camaro. Otherwise, engines, transmissions, and option groups stayed the same as in '70½.

In the interior, woodgrain paneling again formed part of the Z-87 and Z-23 packages. The single-bar steering wheel listed RS, SS, and standard Camaro levels, and the 4-spoke, H-bar sport wheel (NK-4; $15.80) continued in black.

1971's Custom interior (Z-87) offered only cloth-with-vinyl seats—cloth on the cushions and backrests in 2-tone weaves of black plus blue, jade, saddle, black, or white. Custom door panels for 1971 were carried over from 1970½ but came in different colors to match the new upholstery materials.

Hidden wipers were again standard in the RS and SS groups. Or you could order the wiper-hiding hood separately as RPO C-24 at $21.10. The Z-28 came with so-called Trans-Am wheels in 15 x 7-inch size, and you could also get a 14 x 7 Rally wheel (ZJ-7; $45.30 per set) for the SS. Two types of full wheelcover were available—PO-1 at $26.35 and Corvette-derived, thin-bladed turbine covers (PO-2) at $84.30. This last was carried over from 1970½.

1972 Camaro & a Bad Year

That year's national price freeze plus a rollback of the 7% federal excise tax around Christmas 1971 gave new-car sales a big lift for 1972. Unfortunately, however, Camaros never had a chance to partake.

On Apr. 7, 1972, the United Auto Workers (UAW) decided to strike General Motors' assembly plant in Norwood, Ohio. Norwood was the home of the F-Car and the only plant then building Camaros and Firebirds.

For 174 days, no cars left the premises. The strike centered on layoffs, and neither the UAW nor GM actually won any concessions during the 25-week walkout.

Dollar losses came to $20 million in unpaid wages, $5 million in strike benefits, $8 million in lost GM profits, and untold millions lost by stymied suppliers. In terms of cars, General Motors estimated that 39,000 Camaros and Firebirds—worth $125 million to dealers—didn't get built.

When the strike finally ended, 1100 partially assembled cars still clogged the lines. They all had to be scrapped because, by the time the Norwood plant reopened on Sept. 27, 1972, the 1973 season was already under way. The '72 cars couldn't meet '73 bumper laws, and it was too expensive to convert them.

And if that weren't enough, General Motors management seriously considered dropping the Camaro and Firebird altogether after 1972. We noted previously that ponycar demand had dwindled since 1967, and the volume of F-Car sales hardly justified keeping the vehicle alive. One thought was to close the Norwood plant and write it off. Even after post-strike production got under way again, the Nova line there got shifted to another plant to protect it from future labor troubles.

Alex C. Mair, who was Chevrolet's chief engineer during this period, was one of the people who lobbied in favor of keeping the F-Car. He was joined by Pontiac chief engineer Bill Collins and other executives from both divisions.

"On the one hand," reflects Mair, "we had a part of the management team of General Motors that was evaluating the proliferation of products. You know, we really *were* supplying a great segment of the market with lots of different types of vehicles. And we had a great deal of work to do on safety and emissions. All this was taxing our facilities dramatically—taxing not only our engineering and manufacturing facilities but also our assembly facilities.

"The expenditures involved made us reconsider the kinds of vehicles we were producing and where they fit. So one proposal called for getting rid of a couple of lines of cars, notably the Camaro and Firebird. Those pressures were strong enough to actually begin the exodus of those two cars.

"Pontiac Motor Div. by that time had developed a very powerful owner loyalty group for the Firebird. The volume wasn't all that high, but the car had a strong following. So did the Camaro. The earlier Trans-Am wins; the Camaros of Penske and Donohue had created a great loyalty. Owners really liked the car.

"This was a period of transition, though, from performance to non-performance. That affected the sales of those two cars. They didn't become stronger; in fact, they went down year by year. So it seemed an ideal time to some to take them out.

"But fortunately," continues Mair, "various people inside Pontiac and Chevrolet kept speaking out in favor of these two cars. We felt it wasn't the right thing to do to drop them. They were viable cars, good cars, and they provided for buyers who wanted cars with precision handling and good looks. Eventually we were able to convince those elements that originally favored dropping the Camaro and Firebird. We were able to sell them. We've discovered since that it was the wise decision.

"But for a while there, we were in a desperate position, because this was not only the strike period but it was also a time when the models changed, and the emission controls and safety items on the 1972 model-year cars weren't acceptable for the 1973 cars. So we had to scrap a lot of materials and a lot of automobiles that were caught in the strike. It was very costly, of course. And it put the F-Car in a teeter-totter position for quite a long time."

The 1972 Camaros themselves differed from 1971 models most noticeably in the grille texture of the straight-across bumper version. Its grille mesh was coarser, having only seven vertical slats instead of the 12 used previously. The Rally Sport front ensemble, though, stayed the same as before.

Horsepower ratings dipped again, but engine and transmission availability remained exactly the same as in 1971. The 396 couldn't be sold in California for 1972,

In 1972, Chevrolet engineers experimented with Schwitzer turbocharger on 6-cylinder Camaro, cut 4.1 sec. off 0-60 time, added 19 mph to ¼-mile speed.

GM seriously considered dropping Camaro after 1972 strike. One motoring journal published an obituary. The '72 standard grille showed coarser mesh.

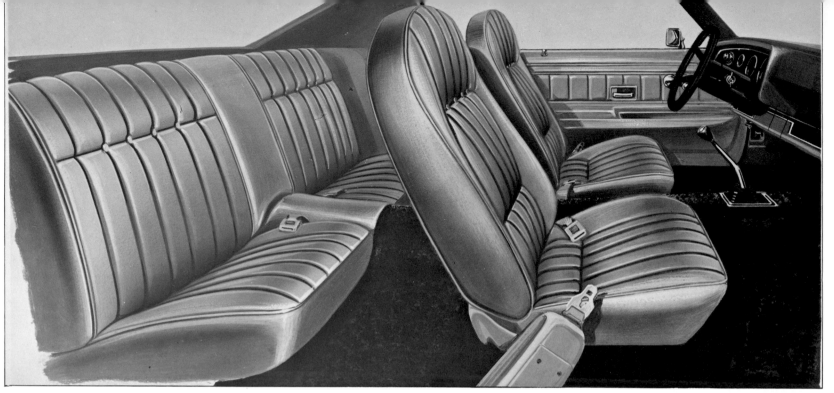

Standard 1973 interior lacks console.   Camaro replaced stirrup shift selector with sticks for all transmissions.   Houndstooth fabric didn't cost extra.

Luxury-touring Type LT bowed in '73, came with hidden wipers, twin mirrors, Rally wheels, and could be combined with Z-28 or RS.

New for '73, polycast Turbine I wheel (left) bonded urethane vanes to steel rim. The Z-28's Trans-Am wheel continued in 15 x 7 size with bright lug nuts, hub, trim ring.

and a new 4-speed shifter came with a reverse lockout (you had to push down and left and forward) plus a different knob.

The Rally Sport (Z-22) no longer incorporated the Style Trim group (Z-21), which you now had to buy separately if you wanted the bright moldings around parking lamps, hood, windows, and inner tail lights. Vinyl roofs for 1972 got the "wet look," and they came in black, white, medium green, light covert (speckle), and medium tan.

Interior packages carried over intact, the Custom group again giving added insulation in the floor, tunnel, and roof areas plus a noise dam between fenders and cowl; also a molded fiberglass blanket under the hood. The Custom interior (Z-87) again offered cloth seat inserts plus woodgraining on the instrument and door panels—and on the console when ordered. The door design changed markedly, with twin map bins in the

armrests and a coin receptacle under the recessed handle.

Front passengers were provided a 3-point shoulder harness for the first time in 1972. This harness changed in detail partway through the model year to meet MVSS requirements. Another interim change during the short 1972 model run was a *Fasten Seat Belt* flasher on the instrument panel.

The 1973 Camaros

The Type LT option arrived in 1973, as did new impact-absorbing bumpers and ratcheting shifter for the Turbo Hydra-Matic to replace the stirrup handle. The door uppers got soft-feel vinyl, the console took on a different silhouette, and the 4-spoke steering wheel, previously RPO NK-4, became standard equipment for all '73 Camaros and would remain so through at least the 1979 model year.

The new Type LT had been suggested by Gertrude

I. (Jimmy) McWilliams, an executive at Chevrolet's advertising agency, Campbell-Ewald. Mrs. McWilliams conceived the Type LT as the top-of-the-line GT offering with a bit more luxury and comfort than the RS or SS and a lot less hair than the Z-28. Engineer Bob Dorn saw the Type LT into production.

When the LT came in, the SS went out. You could, incidentally, combine the Type LT package with the Rally Sport and/or the Z-28 for 1973.

Included in the LT were the 2-barrel, 165-bhp V-8, 7-inch Rally wheels, variable-ratio power steering, hidden wipers, blackout rocker sills and moldings, plus sport mirrors right and left. Inside, you got full instrumentation including tach and clock, extra body and hood insulation, deluxe seat trim, bright-beaded woodgrain on the instrument panel and doors, with LT emblems in the steering hub and on the exterior.

Other option groups continued as before, but the

Type LT came with 145-bhp V-8, variable-ratio power steering, full instruments, specific upholstery, woodgraining, black paint below rocker molding, hood insulation, glovebox lamp.

William L. Mitchell's personalized 1970½ ZL-1 Berlinetta received extensive facelift for 1972, with a soft front end and sloped grille that presaged the 1974 models. The Camaro studio wanted very much to include hidden bumpers and soft facias after '73, but costs stymied them. Inset shows a clay model with simplified soft nose done before Chevrolet decided to go with aluminum bumpers for '74. Jerry Palmer's group kept sloped grille.

Z-28 could be had with Four Seasons air conditioning (C-60; $397) for the first time.

The new 1973 bumpers were quite an engineering tour de force because they met government impact standards and still looked almost the same as before. A square-tube back bar nestled inside the face bar (or bars in the case of the RS), with tubular reinforcing braces, stronger brackets, and rubber-faced guards on all but the Rally Sport. The rear bumpers were similarly strengthened and moved outward from the sheetmetal about a half inch.

Under the hood, Camaro power ratings declined once again. The 396 evaporated, and Powerglide likewise disappeared. But Turbo Hydro became available with the 6 for the first time since 1969. A manual 3-speed was now standard for all 350 V-8's except the Z-28, which

When Chevrolet considered putting rotary engine into downsized '75 Camaro, senior designer John Adams, assistant Ted Schroeder sketched many proposals, including these. Chevy later gave up plans for incorporating the Wankel in Camaro.

continued with the 4-speed as standard and Turbo Hydra-Matic optional.

Interesting new options included the Space-Savr spare (N-65; $14.40), power windows for cars equipped with console (A-31;$75, a midyear release), AM/FM radio with auxiliiary speaker (U-69 and U-80; $135 and $15), and an acoustical package (Z-54; $27) that was standard in the Type LT. Regarding this last, if you wanted the silence of the LT at a considerably lower price, this was the route to go, because the LT listed for $479 above the standard Camaro.

Some interesting new wheels and wheelcovers made their appearance this year. The Rally wheel, RPO ZJ-7 and standard on the LT, was carried over and listed for $44. The Z-28 continued with the Trans-Am 15 x 7 wheel with bright lug nuts, a special spinner, and trim ring. Then you could also get a new Turbine I wheel (PE-1; $110.50) which the Camaro now shared with the big Chevrolet; a new PO-1 wheelcover shared with the

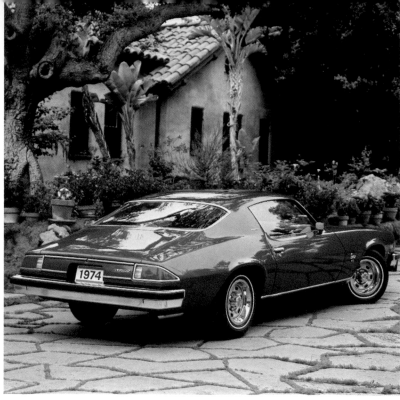

Aluminum bumpers for '74 brought Camaro's first big styling revisions since '70½. Fiberglass tail panel, wraparound lamps dominated rear, while molded

one-piece SMC front cap altered facial expression. Headlamps and parkers peered from recessed "sugar scoops;" bumpers had rubber strips.

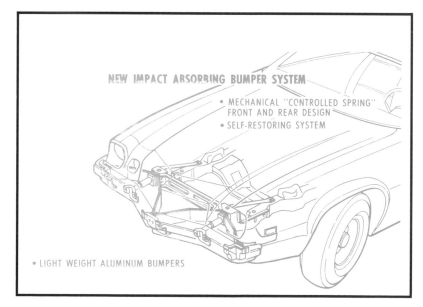

NEW IMPACT ABSORBING BUMPER SYSTEM

• MECHANICAL "CONTROLLED SPRING" FRONT AND REAR DESIGN
• SELF-RESTORING SYSTEM

• LIGHT WEIGHT ALUMINUM BUMPERS

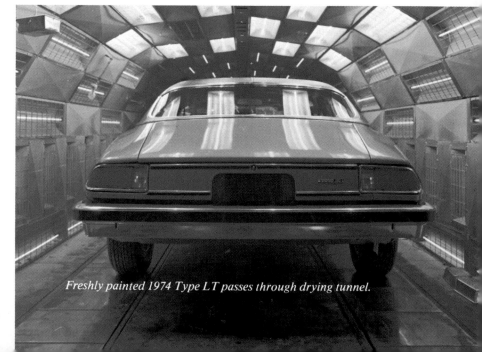

Freshly painted 1974 Type LT passes through drying tunnel.

Production at Norwood plant increased with growing Camaro demand. More capacity came with return to F-Car assembly by Van Nuys plant.

Type LT interior for 1974 combined cord-ridge or knit-vinyl fabrics with full vinyl trim. One-piece molded sail panels with built-in armrests continued.

HEI distributors (high-energy ignition) began in mid-1974 with Z-28's, then expanded to all Camaros by 1975, and integrated coil in cap by '78 model.

Nova and full-sized Chevy; and a simulated wire wheelcover, N-95; $82, that was likewise shared with the big Chevy and Nova.

The Turbine I wheel came with a finned urethane face bonded to a steel hub and rim. A special urethane paint, sprayed on the finned portion, gave the look of cast aluminum. Finishing touches included a peripheral trim ring and a stamped hubcap with brushed face.

Also new and distinguishing for 1973: three more vinyl roof colors, heavier door side beams, full-foam rear seats with one-piece backrest, grey suede finish for the standard instrument cluster, EGR for all engines, and a coolant-recovery system for the radiator, easier-to-use shoulder harness with buzzer sounding only in gear, a revised wiper/washer switch, and rubber trunk mat with felt backing.

Camaros for 1974

Back in 1972, when John DeLorean still managed Chevrolet, the decision had to be made on meeting the much stiffer 1974 federal bumper laws. DeLorean had a number of choices, and he chose to go with a system that incorporated extruded aluminum face bars supported on flat leaf springs.

This decision dramatically affected the 1974 Camaro's styling and brought about the first big fore-and-aft appearance changes since the new body style's arrival in 1970½.

The 1974 Camaro became seven inches longer overall because of the aluminum bumpers, which meant that the grille had to slope forward to meet the front bar. Jerry Palmer's design group incorporated some of the flavor of Bill Mitchell's 1973 Berlinetta in the 1974 Camaro's facial expression.

The '74's front panel was formed from two moldings of a reinforced plastic material called SMC (sheet molded compound). The upper molding, or header panel, incorporated the grille. Headlight bezels, dubbed "sugar scoops" by the stylists, became zinc-alloy castings.

The lower valence panel, also of SMC, wrapped around the bottom corners of both fenders and blended into the wheel cutouts. Parking lamps went into the cat-

walks and had miniature sugar scoops. The SMC area just behind the front bumper mated to a flexible filler panel that, on impact, let the bumper blade move back about two inches without damaging any rigid structure.

Around at the rear, Camaros took on an entirely different aspect for 1974, again to accommodate the new aluminum bumpers. Palmer's group laid an outer trunk end panel over the original one (if you look inside the trunk of any late-model Camaro you'll see the early inner panel still there), and then added cut-in, wraparound, wedge-shaped tail lamps that eliminated the need for rear sidemarkers. All considered, the 1974's major facelift came off remarkably well.

A great number of detail changes marked the 1974 Camaro, including a much plusher rendition of the Type LT. The LT came away with revamped seats and door trim, cord-ridge fabrics or knit vinyl, new woodgrain treatments, and color-coordinated instrument panel, steering wheel, and column.

The LT's insulation now extended to Amberlite blankets inside both doors, in the rear quarters and

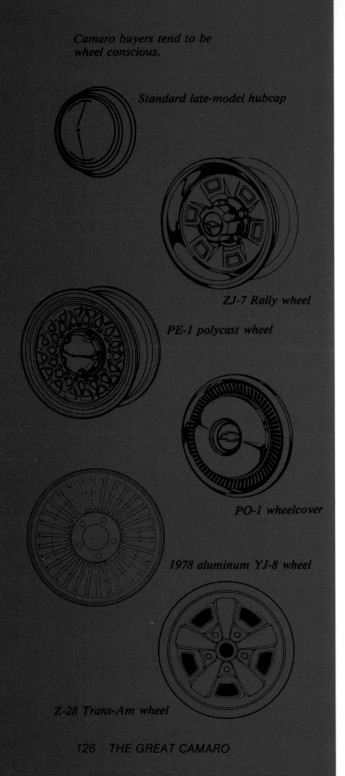

Standard late-model hubcap

ZJ-7 Rally wheel

PE-1 polycast wheel

PO-1 wheelcover

1978 aluminum YJ-8 wheel

Z-28 Trans-Am wheel

Front subframe and rear-suspension isolation help smooth all Camaros' ride.

roof/sail-panel areas, under the carpeting, behind the rear seatback, and under the package shelf.

On the mechanical side, the 307 V-8 was dropped and the 145-bhp 350 became the base V-8. Power steering also became standard with all V-8's, and a magnet inside the pump picked up loose metal filings. Reshaping the gas tank gave three more gallons' capacity (21 instead of 18), and the bumper jack went to a tab-in-slot type. Wear indicators appeared on the front disc brakes and ball joints.

In mid-1974, the Z-28 took on HEI (high-energy ignition), and vinyl roof colors were once more expanded, this time to include 10 hues and textures.

The baby-Moon-like hubcaps for 1973 went to an aluminum cap for '74, with a peaked center. The Camaro now shared this base hubcap with Novas and full-sized Chevrolets. All other Camaro wheels and covers continued from 1973.

The 1975 Camaros

Rumors kept cropping up in auto industry publications that the Camaro would come out with a smaller, all-new body for 1975, based on the Vega shell and incorporting the GMRE —the General Motors rotary engine; the Wankel.

Chevrolet's specifications sheets for 1975 include spaces for the Z-28, but they were never filled in, indicating that the decision to drop the Z after 1974 came at the last minute. For 1975½, though, Chevy decided to re-introduce the Rally Sport option. They renumbered it RPO Z-85 and listed the price at $238.

The most visible styling change for the 1975 model was its larger rear window. The Camaro design studio had toyed with this design since the second generation's conception, but it took until 1975 to make production. Otherwise, body differences between 1974 and '75 were subtle.

One quantum leap, though, involved the paint treatment on the revived 1975½ Rally Sport. Low-gloss black covered the hood, upper fenders, and roof, with a tricolor vinyl band separating the black from the body color. The 1975½ RS, which could be combined with the Type LT, marked the beginning of an extremely successful use of decal striping, blackouts, and colors to bring attention to the latter-day Camaro. The RS came in five 2-tone combinations, all with flat black: metallic blue, light red, silver, antique white, and bright yellow.

The RS's sugar scoops, grille, trunk panel, sport mirrors, and rocker areas were all blacked out. There was very little bright trim on the exterior—only beads around the grille and headlamp bezels. The RS thus

Revived Rally Sport for 1975½ combined low-gloss black paint on roof, hood, tail panel with five primary body colors.

Landau roof treatment was possible with bigger rear window that got its start in '75 model year.

Stick shift for automatic carried thumb reverse lockout. Power window buttons stood on console.

Two new stereo tape systems were added in mid-1975, including this AM/FM unit priced at $363.

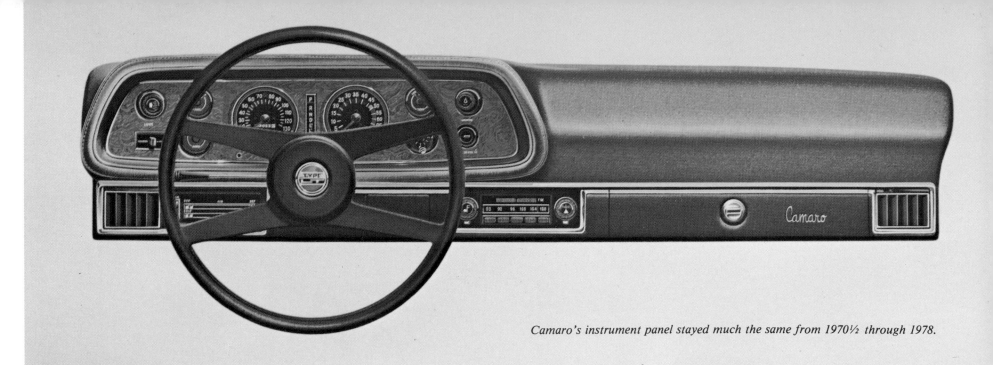

Camaro's instrument panel stayed much the same from 1970½ through 1978.

Applied armrests signify up-option trim level of late-model interiors, with pull below door handle.

Central locking system initially made its appearance in 1975, has proved popular factory option.

N-33 Comfortilt steering column adjusted to six settings, cost $57 extra, was supplied by Saginaw.

Former Olds engineer Bill Mitchell (no kin to retired design v.p. William L.) builds turbocharged small-block Camaros in his Connecticut shop, outfits them with all performance, luxury, hand- *ling goodies, many of his own making; e.g. front air dam. His suppliers include AiResearch, Koni, Recaro, Minilite.*

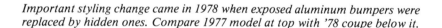

Important styling change came in 1978 when exposed aluminum bumpers were replaced by hidden ones. Compare 1977 model at top with '78 coupe below it.

Rear speaker flanks air-conditioner outlet on late-model package shelf (top). Cloth inserts on door panels plus carpeted lower trim mark Custom interiors.

again became an *exterior* appearance package only. A lot of buyers, though, ordered the optional spoiler and the new-for-1975 Gymkhana suspension.

The Gymkhana suspension (Z-86; $66 with RS and LT, $112 with others) included 15 x 7-inch ZJ-7 Rally wheels with E60-15 white-letter tires, front and rear stabilizer bars, revalved heavy-duty shocks, and fast-ratio steering. A spin-off of the Z-86, the Radial Tuned suspension package (FE-8; $35), deleted the Rally wheels and fast steering but included everything else. Steel-belted radial tires, which became standard for 1975, didn't require the Radial Tuned suspension option, however.

Early in the model year, a new exterior package called Sports Decor (RPO Z-08) had been introduced. It included body-color mirrors, door handle paint inserts, and a body-color vinyl applique on the lower front and rear bumpers. You could get it with any Camaro, including the LT. This package, though, was withdrawn

in midyear. And the LT's major change was the use of birdseye maple woodgraining instead of 1974's meridian walnut.

Catalytic converters were added to all Camaros for 1975, as were finned rear brake drums, twin-exhaust mufflers for all V-8's, and the HEI system, previously available only in the Z-28.

Interesting options this year included power door locks, and in 1975½ cruise control became available, as did air conditioning for the 6, two new tape players with AM/FM stereo, and a deep-pile carpet option. A dash-mounted fuel economy indicator had been slated for midyear but got cancelled at the last minute.

The 1976 Camaros

The Camaro's base V-8 for 1976 became a new 305 instead of the previous year's 350. Engine selection fell to an all-time low—only three powerplants available. Power brakes became standard, and bigger brake wheel

cylinders with improved lining materials rounded out the season's mechanical changes.

The Type LT received a new brushed aluminum trunk panel plus a leather-look instrument background, the tan leather applique replacing 1975's birdseye maple woodgraining. The base instrument panel, meanwhile, carried recessed dials in a clean, white plastic background. A voltmeter replaced the ammeter or telltale used before.

Interior treatments turned out very differently for '76. There were basically three distinct bucket-seat and door-panel styles. The base coupe used the old high-back, rounded seats but with cloth inserts. The base door panel was a modified version of the 1975 design, with an integral armrest and a waffled upper plus new colors.

Then the Type LT moved into two distinct styles, depending on whether the seats were upholstered in cloth or vinyl. The LT seat design was new, with longitudinal sew lines and squared-off headrests. Door panels in two styles had tack-on armrests combined with pull handles: plain panel faces for interiors with cloth seats and pleated faces for interiors with vinyl seats.

The polycast Turbine I wheel was replaced with a new urethane/steel wheel that had multi-pointed spokes radiating from a "5-lug" hubcap. And the Rally wheels, standard on the LT, were available in both 14 x 6 and 14 x 7 sizes.

A Sport Roof treatment, with a body-color basket handle over the rear portion and a vinyl insert over the passenger area, became a new option for 1976. It cost $96 but didn't list an RPO number. The vinyl roof came in seven colors.

The year 1976 marked a return of the F-Car to the Van Nuys, Calif., assembly plant. Camaros and Firebirds had originally been built in Van Nuys from 1967 through 1971. Startup began again in early 1976. Assembly at Norwood, Ohio, continued throughout the F-Car's life—with the exception of the 174-day 1972 strike. In 1978, Van Nuys had the capacity to produce 60 cars an hour, while Norwood's capacity was 55 cars per hour. Both plants normally worked two shifts.

Camaro for 1977

Except for hidden wipers becoming standard for all 1977 Camaros, there was relatively little change in the beginning of the model year. The big news waited until 1977½, when the new Z-28 reappeared (see Chapter Six). The man primarily responsible for resurrecting the Z was Camaro chief engineer Tom Zimmer. Zimmer noted the great popularity of Pontiac's Firebird Trans-Am and convinced Chevrolet management that the Camaro needed a direct T-A rival.

We won't repeat the 1977½ Z-28 story, but we'll touch on the subtle differences in the 1977 line as a whole. For example, the 4-speed transmission repositioned reverse gear from far-left-up to far-left-down.

The Type LT received a new interior fabric called Radcliffe woven sport cloth, which replaced the 1976 plaid material. Grained, single-tone vinyl continued.

And for 1977, the expense of inflating the Space-Savr spare was cut in half by eliminating the old throwaway freon cannister and replacing it with a rechargeable CO_2 cylinder. The carbon dioxide cylinder pressure at below-zero temperatures was also about double that of the freon cannister.

The 1978 Camaros

The 1978 Camaro had been in the wings since 1974. "We had designed the soft fronts and rears for the Camaro way back in 1974," comments designer Jerry Palmer. "We based them partly on Bill Mitchell's ZL-1 Berlinetta showcar. Now that car, which had the soft front and rear, proved to be a very useful tool for doing the 1978 models—not only in design but also to help sell the ideas to our management. The 1973 Berlinetta had

It's interesting to compare 1977 and '78 rear treatments. The '77 sets license above exposed aluminum bumper. The 1978 models at left and below sport vinyl-covered, body-color bumpers, big tri-color tail lamps. Z-28 uses black trim instead of bright moldings.

For 1979, Type LT was replaced by Berlinetta, which took PE-1 wheels as standard. Wheels came with body-color backgrounds.

quite a bit of exposure at autoshows and also with GM brass.

"So keeping in mind that Pontiac was gaining momentum in everything they were doing in soft facias, Chevrolet finally woke up and decidedly got the message. So the 1973 Berlinetta became sort of a theme car for the 1978 model. Not that it was initially intended to come out that late. We'd originally hoped to have it out for 1976, then 1977, and we finally made it in 1978."

To go along with the soft, bumper-hiding front ensemble, new rear graphics accented the much larger,

tricolor, wedge-shaped tail lamps, with their black outlines and black or argent central trunk panels. The rear license moved to the lower bumper pan instead of resting in an open doorway in the middle of the trunk panel.

Inside, the 1978 Camaros' interior colors went from five to six, three being new: dark green, camel, and carmine. Bayonne woven cloth, Edinburgh sport cloth in black only, and Rattan vinyl became new for 1978. Door trim panels and the cloth seat design were new for the standard Camaro, but the vinyl seat design was carried over. Door trim panels in the Type LT were again

restyled. The Z-28 got a simulated string-wrapped steering wheel.

In Van Nuys, on May 11, 1978, the two millionth Camaro rolled off the assembly line—a gold coupe. Chevrolet general manager Robert D. Lund was on hand for the ceremonies.

The Camaro T-top option entered production in the winter of '78, with grey-tinted glass in lift-out panels. And a new optional road wheel, the YJ-8, became available for all models. For the Z-28, the YJ-8 wheel came in 15 x 7-inch size and was offered in gold or silver only, with Z-28 emblems on the hubs.

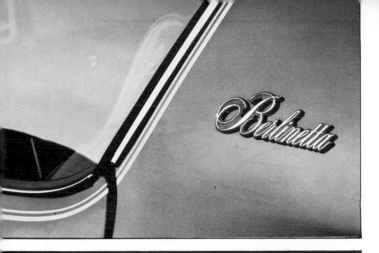

Fisher made T-tops for the first time in 1979. That year's Camaros shared revised dashboard.

Berlinetta (top) boasted pinstripe highlights around side windows and backlight. Rally Sport (bottom) continued for '79, but in more colors. Engine choices remained 250-cid 6, 305 V-8, and two 4-barrel 350's.

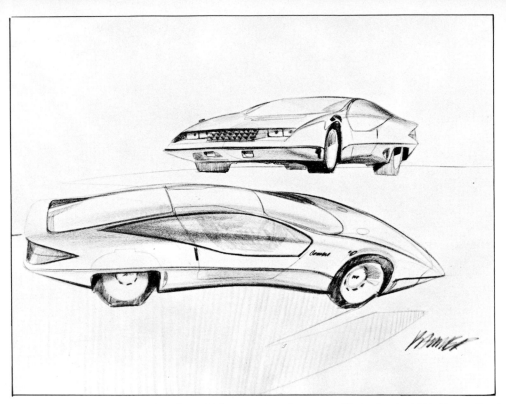

Looking ahead to third-generation Camaros, likely due in 1981-82, studio head Jerry Palmer offers these possibilities—probably with fwd and V-6 power.

(Below) *Camaro senior designer John Adams had the same time frame in mind when he sketched futuristic Rally Sports. Adams tried to preserve family identity.*

Taking the 1981-82 Camaros a step beyond sketches, Palmer's studio has been developing scale models, including handsome coupe shown above and below.

Another new wheel, the redone ZJ-7, looked much like the earlier Rally wheels but had body-color paint in the slot areas. It was standard on the LT and came in 13 different colors.

The 1978 HEI system integrated the coil into the distributor cap for the first time on all engines. Camaro engineers added frame reinforcements to the front end to tie the frame into the crossmember. The 305 V-8 now came with a 4-speed as its standard transmission instead of the old 3-speed.

Camaros for 1978 still came in five basic levels of trim: the base coupe; the Style Trim package (Z-21; $70); Type LT ($315 above base); Rally Sport (Z-85; $370); and the Z-28 ($1189 additional). The LT could again be combined with the Rally Sport, and that meant a saving of $119 over buying each package separately. A lot of equipment in both duplicated, of course.

Camaros for 1979

After tossing around the name Berlinetta for the Camaro since 1969, Chevrolet finally announced a production version 10 years later. The 1979 Berlinetta

replaced the Type LT and became an even more luxurious extension of it.

Most of the features of the LT were carried into the Berlinetta, including dual mirrors, special wheels, paint, emblems, and interior. The PE-1 polycast wheels from 1976 became standard on the Berlinetta, but with color-keyed inners. The aluminum YJ-8 wheels from 1978 were listed as optional.

The Camaro's instrument panel had remained basically unchanged since the car's inception, but it did change for 1979. "The old tools were worn out from making so many panels," said Camaro studio head Jerry Palmer. "So we got word that if we were able to re-do the panel at a cost saving, we could. One of the things we had to remember was to keep the same instrument cluster as before—we had to work with the same instruments. So I think Bill Scott, the fellow who designed the 1979 panel, did a pretty nice job of cleaning it up and adding some newness."

Relatively little else changed for 1979 except for the Z-28's graphics, which we've detailed in Chapter Six.

The Camaro's place in the pantheon of cars seems assured now for all time. Certain first-generation models are already highly prized by collectors, particularly Z-28's, convertibles, pace cars, and clean examples. The early second-generation Z-28's are likewise beginning to pique collector interest.

Camaros have always been sought-after on the used car market. CAR & DRIVER once ranked them second only to Corvettes as holding their resale value. And as time passes, more and more Camaros from every year and model will enter the arena of the collectable.

During the Camaro's Development and Existence

Chevrolet General Managers

Name	Tenure	Later became
S.E. Knudsen	11/1/61—6/30/65	Chairman, White Motor Co.
E.M. Estes	7/1/65—1/31/69	President, General Motors
J.Z. DeLorean	2/1/69—9/30/72	Founder, DeLorean Motor Corp.
F.J. McDonald	10/1/72—10/31/74	V.P. & Dir., General Motors
R.D. Lund	11/1/74—present	

Chevrolet Chief Engineers

E.J. Premo	3/1/63—7/31/66	(Retired)
A.C. Mair	8/1/66—9/30/72	General Mgr., Pontiac Div.
D.H. McPherson	10/1/72—9/30/75	General Mgr., GM of Canada
R.C. Stempel	10/1/75—present	

Dealer Introduction Dates

Model year	Camaro	Firebird	Mustang
1967	9/29/66	2/23/67	9/30/66
1968	9/21/67	9/21/67	9/22/67
1969	9/26/68	9/26/68	9/27/68
1970	2/26/70	2/26/70	9/19/69
1971	9/29/70	9/29/70	9/18/70
1972	9/23/71	9/23/71	9/24/71
1973	9/21/72	9/21/72	9/22/72
1974	9/20/73	9/20/73	9/21/73
1975	9/27/74	9/27/74	9/27/74
1976	10/2/75	9/25/75	10/3/75
1977	9/30/76	9/30/76	10/1/76
1978	10/6/77	10/6/77	10/7/77
1979	9/21/78	9/21/78	10/6/78

Source: *Ward's* Annuals and *Automotive News* Almanacs.

Camaro Model-Year Production

Year	Total Prod'n	Domestic	Export	Rally Sport	Super Sport	Z-28	V-8 Engine	6-cyl	3-spd. trans.	4-spd. trans.	Autom. trans.	Air cond.	Power steering	Power windows
1967	220,917	207,049	13,868	64,842	34,411	602	162,109	58,808	49,198	47,539	124,180	28,226	92,181	4,957
1968	235,151	222,154	12,997	40,977	27,844	7,199	184,178	50,937	54,948	47,572	132,631	35,866	115,280	3,304
1969*	243,095	230,779	12,316	37,773	33,980	19,014	178,087	65,008	72,395	50,128	120,572	37,878	120,060	2,913
1970½	124,889	117,604	7,295	27,136	12,476	8,733	112,323	12,566	14,859	18,678	91,352	38,565	92,640	N.o.
1971	114,643	107,496	7,147	18,404	8,377	4,862	103,452	11,191	13,042	10,614	90,987	42,537	93,163	N.o.
1972	68,656	64,958	3,698	11,364	6,562	2,575	63,832	4,824	6,053	5,835	56,768	31,737	59,857	N.o.
1973	96,756	89,988	6,768	16,133	N.o.	11,574	93,138	3,618	5,964	11,388	79,404	49,504	96,752	217
1974	151,008	146,596	4,412	N.o.	N.o.	13,802	128,810	22,198	11,174	11,175	128,659	79,279	151,008	N.o.
1975	145,789	141,629	4,160	7,000	N.o.	N.o.	116,430	29,359	10,568	8,688	126,533	77,290	145,755	10,598
1976	182,981	178,741	4,240	15,855	N.o.	N.o.	144,934	38,047	11,440	11,396	160,145	110,901	182,981	18,984
1977	218,854	214,776	4,078	17,026	N.o.	14,349	187,464	31,390	8,811	13,537	196,506	144,443	218,854	31,028
1978	272,633	266,807	5,826	No other figures available for 1978 model year at presstime.										

*Includes 1970 carryover of 1969 design. Camaro convertible production is as follows: 1967, 25,141; 1968, 20,440; 1969-70, 17,573. Total 1969 Special Indy Sport convertible production was 3675. Approximately 100 Indianapolis pace car replica convertibles were produced in 1967. Note: "N.o." means "Not offered."

Credits: The publisher thanks the following individuals and institutions for assistance in preparing this book: Noland Adams, George Angersbach, Autoweek, Jane Barrett, Art Baske, Leon Beauchemin, Bill Sandy Direct Marketing Inc., Alice Bixler, Al Bloemker, Don Bok, John R. Bond, James J. Bradley, Ed Brennan, California Z-28 Assn., Camaro Club of America, Camaros Ltd. of Southern California, Campbell-Ewald Co., CBS Publications, Chevrolet Motor Div., Joie Chitwood Thrill Shows, Larry Colwell, Corvair Club of America, Dodd Mead Co., John Z. DeLorean, Gerald M. Desmond, Bob D'Olivo, Robert Dorn, Ralph Dunwoodie, Elliott M. Estes, Steve Gegner, Larry Givens, Jeffrey I. Godshall, Walter R. Haessner, Haessner Publishing Co., Jack W. Hakspacher, Henry G. Haga, Harrah's Automobile Collection, Steven J. Harris, Bob Hill, Laurel Hiller, David R. Holls, Tony Hopp, Warren Howarth, Bob Hughes, Charles N. Hughes, Image International, Indianapolis Motor Speedway Corp., Gloria Jezewski, Charles M. Jordan, J/Scott Photography, Joseph H. Karshner, Su Kemper, Paul J. King, Semon F. Knudsen, Joseph F. Lang, William Lerg, Alejandro Lewis, Bruce MacDonald, Walter R. Mackenzie, Alex C. Mair, Joan Maki, Ned S. McClurg, W.M. McCollum, David R. McLellan, Donald H. McPherson, Ronald C. Miller, William L. Mitchell, Frank Moelich, Motor Vehicle Manufacturers Assn., John F. Mueller, James G. Musser Jr., Edward L. Nash, National Automotive History Collection at the Detroit Public Library, National Camaro Assn., Dave Newell, Andrew V. O'Keefe, Pierre Ollier, Jerry Palmer, Roger Penske, Petersen Publishing Co., Vince W. Piggins, Pontiac Motor Div., William L. Porter, E.J. Premo, Douglas R. Remy, Road & Track, Bob Rochelle, Charles M. Rubly, Irvin W. Rybicki, Don Schwarz, John Shinella, Lawerence K. Shinoda, Judith Siff, Chuck Smith, Elizabeth L. Smith, Society of Automotive Engineers, Lorin Sorensen, James W. Sponseller, Dick Thompson, James L. Tolley, Ron Tonkin, Bob Tronolone, Jack W. Turner Jr., Don Urban, Victor D. Valade, Paul van Valkenburgh, Jim Wangers, Kay Ward, Ward's Automotive Reports, Bill Warner, Tom Warth, Roger Wickersham, James J. Williams, Don J. Wilson, John A. Wilson, Bob Wingate, James Wren, Wallace A. Wyss, Smokey Yunick, and Tom R. Zimmer. Typesetting by Jeanne Graham. Production by Vanguard Press, Stockton, Calif. Printing and binding by R.R. Donnelley & Sons, Chicago. Art direction by Richard E. Hanson.

1967 Camaro Engines

	CID	Con-fig.	B&S, in.	Bhp @ rpm	Torque @ rpm	Compr. ratio	Carb.
Base	230	I-6	3.875 x 3.25	140 @ 4400	220 @ 1600	8.5:1	1V
L-22	250	I-6	3.875 x 3.53	155 @ 4200	235 @ 1600	8.5:1	1V
Z-28	302	V-8	4.002 x 3.005	290 @ 5800	290 @ 4200	11.0:1	4V
Base	327	V-8	4.00 x 3.25	210 @ 4600	320 @ 2400	8.75:1	2V
L-30	327	V-8	4.00 x 3.25	275 @ 4800	355 @ 3200	10.0:1	4V
L-48	350	V-8	4.00 x 3.48	295 @ 4800	380 @ 3200	10.25:1	4V
L-35	396	V-8	4.094 x 3.76	325 @ 4800	410 @ 3200	10.25:1	4V
L-78	396	V-8	4.094 x 3.76	375 @ 5600	415 @ 3600	11.0:1	4V

1967 Camaro Drivetrains

		Base 230	L-22 250	Z-28 302	Base 327	L-30 327	L-48 350	L-35 396	L-78 396
3-spd. manual transmission ratios	1	2.85:1	2.85:1	N.o.	2.54:1	2.54:1	2.54:1	2.41:1	2.41:1
	2	1.68:1	1.68:1	N.o.	1.50:1	1.50:1	1.50:1	1.57:1	1.57:1
	3	1.00:1	1.00:1	N.o.	1.00:1	1.00:1	1.00:1	1.00:1	1.00:1
	R	2.95:1	2.95:1	N.o.	2.63:1	2.63:1	2.63:1	2.41:1	2.41:1
Clutch diam., in.		9.12	9.12	N.o.	10.4	10.4	11.0	11.0	11.0
Axle ratios	S	3.08:1	3.08:1	N.o.	3.08:1	3.08:1	3.31:1	3.07:1	3.07:1
	E	2.73:1	2.73:1	N.o.	2.73:1	2.73:1	3.07:1	2.73:1	2.73:1
	P	3.55:1	3.55:1	N.o.	3.55:1	3.55:1	3.55:1[b]	3.31:1	3.31:1[b]
4-spd. manual transmission ratios	1	3.11:1	3.11:1	2.20:1	2.54:1	2.54:1	2.52:1	2.52:1	2.20:1
	2	2.20:1	2.20:1	1.64:1	1.80:1	1.80:1	1.88:1	1.88:1	1.64:1
	3	1.47:1	1.47:1	1.27:1	1.44:1	1.44:1	1.47:1	1.47:1	1.27:1
	4	1.00:1	1.00:1	1.00:1	1.00:1	1.00:1	1.00:1	1.00:1	1.00:1
	R	3.11:1	3.11:1	2.26:1	2.54:1	2.54:1	2.59:1	2.59:1	2.26:1
Clutch diam., in.		9.12	9.12	10.4	10.4	10.4	11.0	11.0	11.0
Axle ratios	S	3.08:1	3.08:1	3.73:1	3.08:1	3.08:1	3.31:1	3.07:1	3.07:1
	E	2.73:1	2.73:1	3.07:1	2.73:1	2.73:1	3.07:1	2.73:1	2.73:1
	P	3.55:1	3.55:1	3.31:1[c]	3.55:1	3.55:1	3.55:1[c]	3.31:1	3.31:1[c]
Powerglide transmission ratios	1	1.82:1	1.82:1	N.o.	1.76:1	1.76:1	1.76:1	N.o.	N.o.
	2	1.00:1	1.00:1	N.o.	1.00:1	1.00:1	1.00:1	N.o.	N.o.
	R	1.82:1	1.82:1	N.o.	1.76:1	1.76:1	1.76:1	N.o.	N.o.
Axle ratios	S	2.73:1[e]	2.73:1[e]	N.o.	2.73:1[e]	2.73:1[e]	3.07:1	N.o.	N.o.
	E	N.o.	N.o.	N.o.	N.o.	N.o.	2.73:1	N.o.	N.o.
	P	3.55:1	3.55:1	N.o.	3.55:1	3.55:1	3.31:1[b]	N.o.	N.o.
Turbo Hydra-Matic transmission ratios	1	NOT OFFERED					2.48:1	N.o.	
	2						1.48:1	N.o.	
	3						1.00:1	N.o.	
	R						2.08:1	N.o.	
Axle ratios	S						2.73:1[e]	N.o.	
	E						N.o.	N.o.	
	P						3.07:1	N.o.	

Notes: "S," "E," and "P" under axle ratios stand for "Standard," "Economy," and "Performance." [a]Heavy-duty floorshift 3-speed ratios given; normal 3-speed same as L-30. [b]3.55 and/or 3.73 optional. [c]Optional performance ratios range from 3.55 to 4.88. Positraction required with some low ratios. [d]Alternate 4-speed same as for L-35 396 V-8. [e]RS ratio 3.08; air conditioning uses 3.08 or 3.55 all transmissions. "N.o." means "not offered."

1968 Camaro Engines

	CID	Con-fig.	B&S, in.	Bhp @ rpm	Torque @ rpm	Compr. ratio	Carb.
Base	230	I-6	3.875 x 3.25	140 @ 4400	220 @ 1600	8.50:1	1V
L-22	250	I-6	3.857 x 3.53	155 @ 4200	235 @ 1600	8.50:1	1V
Z-28	302	V-8	4.002 x 3.005	290 @ 5800	290 @ 4200	11.0:1	4V
Base	327	V-8	4.001 x 3.25	210 @ 4600	320 @ 2400	8.75:1	2V
L-30	327	V-8	4.001 x 3.25	275 @ 4800	355 @ 3200	10.0:1	4V
L-48	350	V-8	4.00 x 3.48	295 @ 4000	380 @ 3200	10.25:1	4V
L-35	396	V-8	4.094 x 3.76	325 @ 4800	410 @ 3200	10.25:1	4V
L-34	396	V-8	4.094 x 3.76	350 @ 5200	415 @ 3400	10.25:1	4V
L-78	396	V-8	4.094 x 3.76	375 @ 5600	415 @ 3600	11.0:1	4V
L-89	396	V-8	4.094 x 3.76	375 @ 5600	415 @ 3600	11.0:1	4V

Note: L-89 differed from L-78 by having aluminum heads, larger valves, a specific Holley carburetor, different transmission, etc.

1968 Camaro Drivetrains

		Base 230	L-22 250	Z-28 302	Base 327	L-30 327	L-48 350	L-35 396	L-34 396	L-78 396	L-89 396
3-spd. manual transmission ratios	1	2.85:1	2.85:1	N.o.	2.54:1	2.54:1	2.41:1[a]	2.41:1	2.41:1	2.41:1	2.41:1
	2	1.68:1	1.68:1	N.o.	1.50:1	1.50:1	1.59:1	1.59:1	1.59:1	1.59:1	1.59:1
	3	1.00:1	1.00:1	N.o.	1.00:1	1.00:1	1.00:1	1.00:1	1.00:1	1.00:1	1.00:1
	R	2.95:1	2.95:1	N.o.	2.63:1	2.63:1	2.41:1	2.41:1	2.41:1	2.41:1	2.41:1
Clutch diam., in.		9.12	9.12	N.o.	10.34	10.34	11.0	11.0	11.0	11.0	11.0:1
Axle ratios	S	3.08:1	3.08:1	N.o.	3.08:1	3.08:1	3.31:1	3.07:1	3.31:1	3.55:1	3.55:1
	E	2.73:1	2.73:1	N.o.	2.73:1	2.73:1	3.07:1	2.73:1	3.07:1	3.31:1	3.31:1
	P	3.55:1	3.55:1	N.o.	3.55:1	3.55:1	3.55:1	3.31:1	3.55:1[b]	3.73:1[b]	3.73:1[b]
4-spd. manual transmission ratios	1	2.85:1	2.85:1	2.20:1[c]	2.54:1	2.54:1	2.52:1	2.52:1	2.52:1	2.20:1[c]	2.20:1[c]
	2	2.02:1	2.02:1	1.64:1	1.80:1	1.80:1	1.88:1	1.88:1	1.88:1	1.64:1	1.64:1
	3	1.35:1	1.35:1	1.27:1	1.44:1	1.44:1	1.46:1	1.46:1	1.46:1	1.27:1	1.27:1
	4	1.00:1	1.00:1	1.00:1	1.00:1	1.00:1	1.00:1	1.00:1	1.00:1	1.00:1	1.00:1
	R	2.85:1	2.85:1	2.26:1	2.54:1	2.54:1	2.54:1	2.59:1	2.59:1	2.26:1	2.26:1
Clutch diam., in.		9.12	9.12	10.34	10.34	10.34	11.0	11.0	11.0	11.0	11.0:1
Axle ratios	S	3.08:1	3.08:1	3.73:1	3.08:1	3.08:1	3.31:1	3.07:1	3.31:1	3.55:1	3.55:1
	E	2.73:1	2.73:1	3.07:1[b]	2.73:1	2.73:1	3.07:1[b]	2.73:1	3.07:1[b]	3.31:1[b]	3.31:1[b]
	P	3.55:1	3.55:1	3.31:1[b]	3.55:1	3.55:1	3.55:1[b]	3.31:1	3.55:1[b]	3.73:1[b]	3.73:1[b]
Torque-Drive, Powerglide & Turbo Hydra-Matic transmission ratios	1	1.82:1	1.82:1	N.o.	1.76:1	1.76:1	1.76:1	2.48:1	2.48:1	N.o.	N.o.
	2	1.00:1	1.00:1	N.o.	1.00:1	1.00:1	1.00:1	1.48:1	1.48:1	N.o.	N.o.
	3	—	—	N.o.	—	—	—	1.00:1	1.00:1	N.o.	N.o.
	R	1.82:1	1.82:1	N.o.	1.76:1	1.76:1	1.76:1	2.08:1	2.08:1	N.o.	N.o.
Axle ratios	S	2.73:1[d]	2.73:1[d]	N.o.	2.73:1[d]	2.73:1[d]	3.07:1	2.73:1[d]	3.07:1[d]	N.o.	N.o.
	E	2.56:1	2.56:1	N.o.	2.56:1	2.56:1	2.73:1	2.56:1	2.73:1	N.o.	N.o.
	P	3.55:1	3.55:1	N.o.	3.55:1	3.55:1	3.55:1[b]	3.31:1	3.55:1[b]	N.o.	N.o.

[a]Ratios given are for heavy-duty 3-speed; standard 3-speed also available with same ratios as L-30 327 V-8. [b]Certain performance ratios from 3.55:1 to 4.88:1 optional. [c]Alternate close-ratio 4-speed available with ratios identical to L-48 350 V-8, plus heavy-duty 4-speed with same ratios shown. [d]RS came with 3.07 or 3.08:1 axle ratio.

1969 Camaro Engines

	CID	Config.	B&S, in.	Bhp @ rpm	Torque @ rpm	Compr. ratio	Carb.
Base	230	I-6	3.875 x 3.25	140 @ 4400	220 @ 1600	8.5:1	1V
L-22	250	I-6	3.875 x 3.53	155 @ 4200	235 @ 1600	8.5:1	1V
Z-28	302	V-8	4.002 x 3.005	290 @ 5800	290 @ 4200	11.0:1	4V
Base	307	V-8	3.875 x 3.25	200 @ 4600	300 @ 2400	9.0:1	2V
LF-3	327	V-8	4.00 x 3.25	210 @ 4600	320 @ 4200	8.75:1	2V
L-65	350	V-8	4.00 x 3.48	250 @ 4200	345 @ 2800	9.0:1	2V
L-48	350	V-8	4.00 x 3.48	300 @ 4800	380 @ 3200	10.25:1	4V
L-35	396	V-8	4.094 x 3.76	325 @ 4800	410 @ 3200	10.25:1	4V
L-34	396	V-8	4.094 x 3.76	350 @ 5200	415 @ 3400	10.25:1	4V
L-78	396	V-8	4.094 x 3.76	375 @ 5600	415 @ 3600	11.0:1	4V
L-89	396	V-8	4.094 x 3.76	375 @ 5600	415 @ 3600	11.0:1	4V
ZL-1	427	V-8	4.25 x 3.76	425 @ 5600	460 @ 4000	11.0:1	3-2V

Note: L-89 differed from L-78 in having aluminum heads, larger valves, a specific Holley carburetor, different transmission, etc. LF-3 was superseded by 307 V-8 as 1969's base V-8. Only 50 ZL-1's—the aluminum-block 427—were installed in Camaros by the factory.

1969 Camaro Drivetrains

		Base 230	L-22 250	Z-28 302	Base 307	L-65 350	L-48 350	L-35 396	L-34 396	L-78 396	L-89 396
3-spd. manual transmission ratios	1	2.85:1	2.85:1	N.o.	2.85:1	2.54:1	2.42:1	2.42:1	2.42:1	2.42:1	2.42:1
	2	1.68:1	1.68:1	N.o.	1.68:1	1.50:1	1.58:1	1.58:1	1.58:1	1.58:1	1.58:1
	3	1.00:1	1.00:1	N.o.	1.00:1	1.00:1	1.00:1	1.00:1	1.00:1	1.00:1	1.00:1
	R	2.95:1	2.95:1	N.o.	2.95:1	2.63:1	2.41:1	2.41:1	2.42:1	2.41:1	2.41:1
Clutch diam., in.		9.12	9.12	N.o.	10.34	10.34	11.0	11.0	11.0	11.0	11.0
Axle ratios	S	3.08:1	3.08:1	N.o.	3.08:1	3.08:1	3.31:1	3.07:1	3.31:1	3.55:1	3.55:1
	E	2.73:1	2.73:1	N.o.	2.73:1	2.73:1	3.07:1	2.73:1	3.07:1	3.31:1	3.31:1
	P	3.36:1	3.36:1	N.o.	3.36:1	3.36:1	3.55:1[a]	3.31:1	3.55:1	3.73:1	3.73:1
4-spd. manual transmission ratios	1	2.85:1	2.85:1	2.52:1[b]	2.85:1	2.54:1	2.52:1[b]	2.52:[b]	2.20:1[b]	2.20:1[b]	2.20:1[b]
	2	2.02:1	2.02:1	1.88:1	2.02:1	1.80:1	1.88:1	1.88:1	1.64:1	1.64:1	1.64:1
	3	1.35:1	1.35:1	1.46:1	1.35:1	1.44:1	1.46:1	1.46:1	1.27:1	1.27:1	1.27:1
	4	1.00:1	1.00:1	1.00:1	1.00:1	1.00:1	1.00:1	1.00:1	1.00:1	1.00:1	1.00:1
	R	2.85:1	2.85:1	2.59:1	2.85:1	2.54:1	2.59:1	2.59:1	2.26:1	2.26:1	2.26:1
Clutch diam., in.		9.12	9.12	10.34	10.34	10.34	11.0	11.0	11.0	11.0	11.0
Axle ratios	S	3.08:1	3.08:1	3.73:1	3.08:1	3.08:1	3.31:1	3.07:1	3.31:1	3.55:1	3.55:1
	E	2.73:1	2.73:1	3.55:1	2.73:1	2.73:1	3.07:1	2.73:1	3.07:1	3.31:1	3.31:1
	P	3.36:1	3.36:1	4.10:1[a]	3.36:1	3.36:1	3.55:1[a]	3.31:1	3.55:1[a]	3.73:1[a]	3.73:1[a]
Powerglide transmission ratios	1	1.82:1	1.82:1	N.o.	1.82:1	1.76:1	1.76:1	N.o.	N.o.	N.o.	N.o.
	2	1.00:1	1.00:1	N.o.	1.00:1	1.00:1	1.00:1	N.o.	N.o.	N.o.	N.o.
	R	1.82:1	1.82:1	N.o.	1.82:1	1.76:1	1.76:1	N.o.	N.o.	N.o.	N.o.
Axle ratios	S	2.73:1[c]	2.73:1[c]	N.o.	2.73:1	2.56:1	3.08:1	N.o.	N.o.	N.o.	N.o.
	E	2.56:1	2.56:1	N.o.	2.56:1	—	—	N.o.	N.o.	N.o.	N.o.
	P	3.08:1	3.08:1[a]	N.o.	3.08:1	3.08:1	3.36:1	N.o.	N.o.	N.o.	N.o.
Turbo Hydra-Matic transmission ratios	1	2.52:1	2.52:1	N.o.	2.52:1	2.52:1	2.52:1	2.48:1	2.48:1	2.48:1	2.48:1
	2	1.52:1	1.52:1	N.o.	1.52:1	1.52:1	1.52:1	1.48:1	1.48:1	1.48:1	1.48:1
	3	1.00:1	1.00:1	N.o.	1.00:1	1.00:1	1.00:1	1.00:1	1.00:1	1.00:1	1.00:1
	R	1.93:1	1.93:1	N.o.	1.93:1	1.93:1	1.93:1	2.00:1	2.00:1	2.00:1	2.00:1
Axle ratios	S	2.56:1[c]	2.56:1[c]	N.o.	2.56:1[c]	2.56:1	3.07:1	3.07:1	3.31:1	3.55:1	3.55:1
	E	—	2.73:1	N.o.	—	—	2.73:1	2.73:1	3.07:1	3.31:1	3.31:1
	P	2.73:1[a]	—	N.o.	2.73:1	3.08:1	3.31:1[a]	—[a]	3.55:1[a]	3.73:1	3.73:1[a]
Torque-Drive transmission ratios	1	1.82:1	1.82:1								
	2	1.00:1	1.00:1								
	R	1.82:1	1.82:1								
Axle ratios	S	2.73:1[c]	2.73:1[c]								
	E	2.56:1	2.56:1								
	P	3.08:1	3.08:1[a]								

NOT OFFERED

[a]Certain performance ratios from 3.08:1 to 4.10:1 optional. [b]Four-speed transmissions with the 2.52:1 and 2.20:1 low may be interchanged optionally at no extra cost; 2.20:1 gearbox is the close-ratio unit. [c]Ratios differ for air-conditioned models.

1970½ Camaro Engines

	CID	Config.	B&S, in.	Bhp @ rpm	Torque @ rpm	Compr. ratio	Carb.
Base	250	I-6	3.875 x 3.53	155 @ 4200	235 @ 1600	8.5:1	1V
Base	307	V-8	3.875 x 3.25	200 @ 4600	300 @ 2400	9.0:1	2V
L-65	350	V-8	4.00 x 3.48	250 @ 4800	345 @ 2800	9.0:1	2V
L-48	350	V-8	4.00 x 3.48	300 @ 4800	380 @ 3200	10.25:1	4V
Z-28	350	V-8	4.00 x 3.48	360 @ 6000	380 @ 4000	11.0'1	4V
L-34	396	V-8	4.126 x 3.76	350 @ 5200	415 @ 3400	10.25:1	4V
L-78	396	V-8	4.126 x 3.76	375 @ 5600	415 @ 3600	11.0:1	4V
LS-6	454	V-8	4.251 x 4.00	450 @ 4600	500 @ 3600	11.25:1	4V

Note: Actual displacement of L-34 and L-78 "396" V-8's is 402 cid.

1970½ Camaro Drivetrains

		Base 250	Base 307	L-65 350	L-48 350	Z-28 350	L-34 396	L-78 396	LS-6 454
3- and 4-spd. manual transmission ratios	1	2.85:1	2.85:1	2.54:1	2.52:1	2.52:1[a]	2.20:1[a]	2.52:1[a]	2.20:1[a]
	2	1.68:1	1.68:1	1.80:1	1.88:1	1.88:1	1.64:1	1.88:1	1.64:1
	3	1.00:1	1.00:1	1.44:1	1.46:1	1.46:1	1.27:1	1.46:1	1.27:1
	4			1.00:1	1.00:1	1.00:1	1.00:1	1.00:1	1.00:1
	R	2.95:1	2.95:1	2.54:1	2.59:1	2.59:1	2.26:1	2.59:1	2.26:1
Clutch diam., in.		9.12	10.34	10.34	11.0	11.0	11.0	11.0	11.0
Axle ratios	S	3.08:1	3.08:1	3.36:1	3.31:1	3.37:1	3.31:1	3.55:1	3.31:1
	E	—	—	—	—	—	—	—	—
	P	—	3.08:1	3.36:1	3.31:1	4.10:1	3.31:1	4.10:1	—
Powerglide & Turbo Hydra-Matic transmission ratios	1	1.82:1	1.82:1[b]	2.52:1	2.52:1	2.48:1	2.48:1	N.o.	2.48:1
	2	1.00:1	1.00:1	1.52:1	1.52:1	1.48:1	1.48:1	N.o.	1.48:1
	3	—	—	1.00:1	1.00:1	1.00:1	1.00:1	N.o.	1.00:1
	R	1.82:1	1.82:1	1.93:1	1.93:1	2.08:1	2.08:1	N.o.	2.08:1
Axle ratios	S	2.73:1	2.73:1	2.73:1	3.07:1	3.37:1	3.31:1	N.o.	3.31:1
	E	—	—	—	—	—	—	N.o.	—
	P	—	—	3.31:1	3.07:1	4.10:1	3.31:1	N.o.	—

Note: Only manual transmission available with base 250 and 307 was the 3-speed. Only manual transmission for larger V-8's were 4-speeds. [a]Alternate 4-speed transmissions offered at no extra cost. [b]Turbo Hydra-Matic with 2.52:1 low range was also available for the 307 V-8.

1971 Camaro Engines

	CID	Con-fig.	B&S, in.	Gross Bhp @ rpm	Net Bhp @ rpm	Gross torque @ rpm	Net torque @ rpm	Compr. Ratio	Carb.
Base	250	I-6	3.875 x 3.53	145 @ 4200	110 @ 3800	230 @ 1600	185 @ 1600	8.5:1	1V
Base	307	V-8	3.875 x 3.25	200 @ 4600	140 @ 4400	300 @ 2400	235 @ 2400	8.5:1	2V
L-65	350	V-8	4.00 x 3.48	245 @ 4800	165 @ 4000	350 @ 2800	280 @ 2400	8.5:1	2V
L-48	350	V-8	4.00 x 3.48	270 @ 4800	210 @ 4400	360 @ 3200	300 @ 2800	8.5:1	4V
Z-28	350	V-8	4.00 x 3.48	330 @ 5600	275 @ 5600	360 @ 4000	300 @ 4000	9.0:1	4V
LS-3	396	V-8	4.126 x 3.76	300 @ 4800	260 @ 4400	400 @ 3200	345 @ 3200	8.5:1	4V

Notes: 1971 was the year GM lowered compression ratios and began to record horsepower and torque in terms of "net" instead of "gross." See text for explanation. As before, the LS-3 "396" V-8 actually displaced 402 cid.

1971 Camaro Drivetrains

		Base 250	Base 307	L-65 350	L-48 350	Z-28 350	LS-3 396
3- and 4-spd.	1	2.85:1	2.85:1	2.54:1	2.52:1	2.52:1	2.20:1
manual transmission	2	1.68:1	1.68:1	1.80:1	1.88:1	1.88:1	1.64:1
ratios	3	1.00:1	1.00:1	1.44:1	1.46:1	1.46:1	1.27:1
	4	—	—	1.00:1	1.00:1	1.00:1	1.00:1
	R	2.95:1	2.95:1	2.54:1	2.59:1	2.59:1	2.26:1
Clutch diam., in.		9.12	10.34	10.34	11.0	11.0	11.0
Axle ratios	S	3.08:1	3.08:1	3.08:1	3.42:1	3.73:1	3.42:1
	E	—	—	—	—	—	—
	P	—	—	—	—	4.10:1	—
Powerglide & Turbo	1	1.82:1	1.82:1[a]	2.52:1	2.52:1	2.48:1	2.48:1
Hydra-Matic	2	1.00:1	1.00:1	1.52:1	1.52:1	1.48:1	1.48:1
transmission ratios	3			1.00:1	1.00:1	1.00:1	1.00:1
	R	1.82:1	1.82:1	1.93:1	1.93:1	2.08:1	2.08:1
Axle ratios	S	3.08:1	3.08:1	2.73:1	3.08:1	3.73:1	3.42:1
	E	—	—	—	—	—	—
	P	—	—	3.42:1	—	4.10:1	—

Note: Only manual transmission available with base 250 and 307 was the 3-speed. Only manual transmission for larger V-8's were 4-speeds. [a]Turbo Hydra-Matic with 2.52:1 low also available with 307 V-8.

1972 Camaro Engines

	CID	Con-fig.	B&S, in.	Bhp @ rpm	Torque @ rpm	Compr. ratio	Carb.
Base	250	I-6	3.875 x 3.53	110 @ 3800	185 @ 1600	8.5:1	1V
Base	307	V-8	3.875 x 3.25	130 @ 4000	230 @ 2400	8.5:1	2V
L-65	350	V-8	4.00 x 3.48	165 @ 4000	280 @ 2400	8.5:1	2V
L-48	350	V-8	4.00 x 3.48	200 @ 4400	300 @ 2800	8.5:1	4V
Z-28	350	V-8	4.00 x 3.48	255 @ 5600	280 @ 4000	9.0:1	4V
LS-3	396	V-8	4.126 x 3.76	240 @ 4400	345 @ 3200	8.5:1	4V

Notes: Horsepower and torque figures listed are net. GM published no gross ratings after 1971 model year. Base 307 and LS-3 "396" not available in California. Base V-8 for California was L-65 350. The LS-3 "396" V-8's actual displacement was 402 cid.

1972 Camaro Drivetrains

		Base 250	Base 307	L-65 350	L-48 350	Z-28 350	LS-3 396
3- and 4-spd. manual	1	2.85:1	2.85:1	2.54:1[a]	2.54:1	2.52:1	2.20:1
transmission ratios	2	1.68:1	1.68:1	1.50:1	1.80:1	1.88:1	1.64:1
	3	1.00:1	1.00:1	1.00:1	1.44:1	1.46:1	1.27:1
	4	—	—	—	1.00:1	1.00:1	1.00:1
	R	2.95:1	2.95:1	2.63:1	2.54:1	2.59:1	2.26:1
Clutch diam., in.		9.12	10.34	10.34	10.34	11.0	11.0
Axle ratios	S	3.08:1	3.08:1	3.08:1	3.42:1	3.73:1[b]	3.42:1[b]
	E	—	—	—	—	—	—
	P	—	—	—	—	4.10:1	—
Powerglide & Turbo	1	1.82:1	1.82:1[a]	2.52:1	2.52:1	2.48:1	2.48:1
Hydra-Matic	2	1.00:1	1.00:1	1.52:1	1.52:1	1.48:1	1.48:1
transmission ratios	3			1.00:1	1.00:1	1.00:1	1.00:1
	R	1.82:1	1.82:1	1.90:1	1.90:1	2.08:1	2.08:1
Axle ratios	S	3.08:1	3.08:1	2.73:1	3.08:1	3.73:1	3.42:1
	E	—	—	—	—	—	—
	P	—	—	3.42:1	—	4.10:1	—

Note: Three-speed manual available only with 250 and 307; 4-speeds only with 350 and 396 V-8's. [a]Turbo Hydra-Matic with 2.52:1 low also available with 307 V-8.

1973 Camaro Engines

	CID	Con-fig.	B&S, in.	Bhp @ rpm	Torque @ rpm	Compr. ratio	Carb.
Base	250	I-6	3.875 x 3.53	100 @ 3600	175 @ 1600	8.25:1	1V
Base	307	V-8	3.875 x 3.25	115 @ 3600	205 @ 2000	8.5:1	2V
L-65	350	V-8	4.00 x 3.48	145 @ 2400	255 @ 2400	8.5:1	2V
L-48	350	V-8	4.00 x 3.48	175 @ 4000	260 @ 2800	8.5:1	4V
Z-28	350	V-8	4.00 x 3.48	245 @ 5200	280 @ 4000	9.0:1	4V

Note: L-65 350 was base V-8 for Type LT package.

1973 Camaro Drivetrains

		Base	Base	L-65	L-48	Z-28
3-spd. manual transmission ratios	1	2.85:1	2.85:1	2.54:1	2.54:1	N.o.
	2	1.68:1	1.68:1	1.50:1	1.50:1	N.o.
	3	1.00:1	1.00:1	1.00:1	1.00:1	N.o.
	R	2.95:1	2.95:1	2.63:1	2.63:1	N.o.
Clutch diam., in		9.12	10.34	10.34	10.34	N.o.
Axle ratios	S	3.08:1	3.08:1	3.08:1	3.08:1	N.o.
	E	—	—	—	—	—
	P	—	—	—	—	—
4-spd. manual transmission ratios	1	N.o.	N.o.	2.54:1	2.54:1	2.52:1[a]
	2	N.o.	N.o.	1.80:1	1.80:1	1.88:1
	3	N.o.	N.o.	1.44:1	1.44:1	1.46:1
	4	N.o.	N.o.	1.00:1	1.00:1	1.00:1
	R	N.o.	N.o.	2.54:1	2.54:1	2.59:1
Clutch diam., in		N.o.	N.o.	10.34	10.34	11.0
Axle ratios	S	N.o.	N.o.	3.08:1	3.42:1	3.73:1
	E	N.o.	N.o.	—	—	3.42:1
	P	N.o.	N.o.	—	—	—
Turbo Hydra-Matic transmission ratios	1	2.52:1	2.52:1	2.52:1	2.52:1	2.48:1
	2	1.52:1	1.52:1	1.52:1	1.52:1	1.48:1
	3	1.00:1	1.00:1	1.00:1	1.00:1	1.00:1
	R	1.93:1	1.93:1	1.93:1	1.93:1	2.08:1
Axle ratios	S	3.08:1	2.73:1	2.73:1	3.08:1	3.73:1
	E	—	—	—	—	—
	P	—	3.42:1	3.42:1	—	3.42:1

[a]Alternate close-ratio 4-speed (2.20:1 low) also offered at no extra cost.

1974 Camaro Engines

	CID	Con-fig.	B&S, in.	Bhp @ rpm	Torque @ rpm	Compr. ratio	Carb.
Base	250	I-6	3.875 x 3.53	100 @ 3600	175 @ 1800	8.25:1	1V
L-65	350	V-8	4.00 x 3.48	145 @ 3800	250 @ 2200	8.5:1	2V
LM-1	350	V-8	4.00 x 3.48	160 @ 3800	250 @ 2400	8.5:1	4V
L-48	350	V-8	4.00 x 3.48	185 @ 4000	270 @ 2600	8.5:1	4V
Z-28	350	V-8	4.00 x 3.48	245 @ 5200	280 @ 4000	9.0:1	4V

Note: L-65 350 V-8 not sold in California; LM-1 was available in California only.

1974 Camaro Drivetrains

		Base 250	L-65 350	LM-1 350	L-48 350	Z-28 350
3-spd. manual transmission ratios	1	2.85:1	2.54:1	2.54:1	2.54:1	N.o.
	2	1.68:1	1.50:1	1.50:1	1.50:1	N.o.
	3	1.00:1	1.00:1	1.00:1	1.00:1	N.o.
	R	2.95:1	2.63:1	2.63:1	2.63:1	N.o.
Clutch diam., in.		9.12	10.34	10.34	10.34	N.o.
Axle ratios	S	3.08:1	3.08:1	3.08:1	3.42:1	N.o.
	E	—	—	—	—	N.o.
	P	—	—	—	—	N.o.

[a]Alternate Z-28 4-speed transmission also available with ratios: 2.43:1, 1.61:1, 1.23:1, 1.00:1, and 2.35:1.

		Base 250	L-65 350	LM-1 350	L-48 350	Z-28 350
4-spd. manual transmission ratios	1	N.o.	2.54:1	2.54:1	2.54:1	2.64:1[a]
	2	N.o.	1.80:1	1.80:1	1.80:1	1.75:1
	3	N.o.	1.44:1	1.44:1	1.44:1	1.33:1
	4	N.o.	1.00:1	1.00:1	1.00:1	1.00:1
	R	N.o.	2.54:1	2.54:1	2.54:1	2.55:1
Clutch diam., in.		N.o.	10.34	10.34	10.34	11.0
Axle ratios	S	N.o.	3.08:1	3.08:1	3.42:1	3.73:1
	E	N.o.	—	—	—	3.42:1
	P	N.o.	—	—	—	3.42:1
Turbo Hydra-Matic transmission ratios	1	2.52:1	2.52:1	2.52:1	2.52:1	2.48:1
	2	1.52:1	1.52:1	1.52:1	1.52:1	1.48:1
	3	1.00:1	1.00:1	1.00:1	1.00:1	1.00:1
	R	1.94:1	1.94:1	1.94:1	1.94:1	2.08:1
Axle ratios	S	3.08:1	2.73:1	2.73:1	3.08:1	3.73:1
	E	—	—	—	—	3.42:1
	P	—	3.42:1	3.42:1	3.42:1	3.73:1

1975 Camaro Engines

	CID	Con-fig	B&S, in.	Bhp @ rpm	Torque @ rpm	Compr. ratio	Carb.
Base	250	I-6	3.875 x 3.53	105 @ 3800	185 @ 1200	8.25:1	1V
L-65	350	V-8	4.00 x 3.48	145 @ 3800	250 @ 2200	8.5:1	2V
LM-1	350	V-8	4.00 x 3.48	155 @ 3800	250 @ 2400	8.5:1	4V

Note: L-65 350 V-8 not available in California.

1975 Camaro Drivetrains

		L-22 250	L-65 350	LM-1 350
3- and 4-spd. manual transmission ratios	1	3.11:1	2.85:1	2.54:1[a]
	2	1.84:1	1.68:1	1.80:1
	3	1.00:1	1.00:1	1.44:1
	4	—	—	1.00:1
	R	3.22:1	2.95:1	2.54:1
Clutch diam., in.		9.12	10.34	10.34
Axle ratios	S	3.08:1	2.73:1	3.08:1
	E	—	2.56:1	—
	P	—	—	—

		L-22 250	L-65 350	LM-1 350
Turbo Hydra-Matic transmission ratios	1	2.52:1	2.52:1	2.52:1
	2	1.52:1	1.52:1	1.52:1
	3	1.00:1	1.00:1	1.00:1
	R	1.93:1	1.93:1	1.93:1
Axle ratios	S	2.73:1	2.73:1	3.08:1
	E	—	2.56:1	2.56:1
	P	3.08:1	—	—

[a]LM-1 came standard with same 3-speed as L-65.

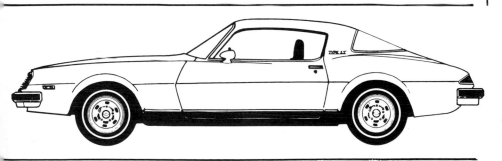

1976 Camaro Engines

	CID	Config.	B&S, in.	Bhp @ rpm	Torque @ rpm	Compr. ratio	Carb.
L-22	250	I-6	3.875 x 3.53	105 @ 3800	185 @ 1200	8.25:1	1V
LG-3	305	V-8	3.736 x 3.48	140 @ 3800	245 @ 2000	8.5:1	2V
LM-1	350	V-8	4.00 x 3.48	165 @ 3800	260 @ 2400	8.5:1	4V

1976 Camaro Drivetrains

		Base 250	LG-3 305	LM-1 350
3- and 4-spd. manual transmission ratios	1	3.11:1	3.11:1	2.85:1[a]
	2	1.84:1	1.84:1	2.02:1
	3	1.00:1	1.00:	1.35:1
	4	—	—	1.00:1
	R	3.22:1	3.22:1	2.85:1
Clutch diam., in		9.12	10.34	10.34
Axle ratios	S	2.73:1	2.73:1	3.08:1
	E	—	—	—
	P	3.08:1	3.08:1	—

		Base 250	LG-3 305	LM-1 350
Turbo Hydra-Matic transmission ratios	1	2.52:1	2.52:1	2.52:1
	2	1.52:1	1.52:1	1.52:1
	3	1.00:1	1.00:1	1.00:1
	R	1.94:1	1.94:1	1.94:1
Axle ratios	S	2.73:1	2.73:1	2.73:1
	E	—	—	—
	P	3.08:1	3.08:1	3.08:1

Note: No manual transmissions available in California for 1976.
[a] Standard transmission for LM-1 is same 3-speed as for LG-3.

1977 Camaro Engines

	CID	Config.	B&S, in.	Bhp @ rpm	Torque @ rpm	Compr. ratio	Carb.
L-22	250*	I-6	3.875 x 3.53	90 @ 3600*	180 @ 1600*	8.3:1	1V
L-22	250	I-6	3.875 x 3.53	110 @ 3800	195 @ 1600	8.3:1	1V
LG-3	305*	V-8	3.736 x 3.48	135 @ 3800*	240 @ 2000*	8.5:1	2V
LG-3	305	V-8	3.736 x 3.48	145 @ 3800	245 @ 2400	8.5:1	2V
LM-1	350*	V-8	4.00 x 3.48	160 @ 3800*	260 @ 2400*	8.5:1	4V
LM-1	350	V-8	4.00 x 3.48	170 @ 3800	270 @ 2400	8.5:1	4V
Z-28	350	V-8	4.00 x 3.48	185 @ 4000	280 @ 2400	8.5:1	4V

*Asterisk denotes California rating.

1977 Camaro Drivetrains

		L-22 250	LG-3 305	LM-1 350	Z-28 350
3-spd. manual transmission ratios	1	3.11:1	3.11:1	3.11:1	3.11:1
	2	1.84:1	1.84:1	1.84:1	1.84:1
	3	1.00:1	1.00:1	1.00:1	1.00:1
	R	3.22:1	3.22:1	3.22:1	3.22:1
Clutch diam., in.		9.12	10.34	10.34	10.34
Axle ratios	S	2.73:1[a]	2.73:1	2.73:1	2.73:1

		L-22 250	LG-3 305	LM-1 350	Z-28 350
4-spd. manual transmission ratios	1	N.o.	N.o.	2.85:1	2.64:1[b]
	2	N.o.	N.o.	2.02:1	1.75:1
	3	N.o.	N.o.	1.35:1	1.34:1
	4	N.o.	N.o.	1.00:1	1.00:1
	R	N.o.	N.o.	2.85:1	2.55:1
Clutch diam., in.		N.o.	N.o.	10.34	10.34
Axle ratios	S	N.o.	N.o.	3.73:1	3.73:1
Turbo Hydra-Matic transmission ratios	1	2.52:1	2.52:1	2.52:1	2.52:1
	2	1.52:1	1.52:1	1.52:1	1.52:1
	3	1.00:1	1.00:1	1.00:1	1.00:1
	R	1.94:1	1.94:1	1.94:1	1.94:1
Axle ratios	S	2.73:1	2.56:1	2.56:1	3.42:1
	E	—	—	—	—
	P	3.08:1	—	3.08:1	—

Note: No manual transmissions available in California for 1977.
[a] Ratio was 3.08:1 with air conditioning. [b] LM-1 4-speed also available in Z-28 in 49 States.

1978 Camaro Engines

	CID	Config.	B&S, in.	Bhp @ rpm	Torque @ rpm	Compr. ratio	Carb.
L-22	250*	I-6	3.875 x 3.53	90 @ 3600*	175 @ 1600*	8.1:1	1V
L-22	250	I-6	3.875 x 3.53	110 @ 3800	190 @ 1600	8.1:1	1V
LG-3	305*	V-8	3.736 x 3.48	135 @ 3800*	240 @ 2000*	8.4:1	2V
LG-3	305	V-8	3.736 x 3.48	145 @ 3800	245 @ 2400	8.4:1	2V
LM-1	350*	V-8	4.00 x 3.48	160 @ 3800	260 @ 2400	8.2:1	4V
LM-1	350	V-8	4.00 x 3.48	170 @ 3800	270 @ 2400	8.2:1	4V
Z-28	350*	V-8	4.00 x 3.48	175 @ 3800*	265 @ 2400*	8.2:1	4V
Z-28	350	V-8	4.00 x 3.48	185 @ 4000	280 @ 2400	8.2:1	4V

*Asterisk denotes California and high-altitude ratings.

1978 Camaro Drivetrains

		L-22 250	LG-3 305	LM-1 350	Z-28 350
3- and 4-spd. manual transmission ratios	1	3.50:1	2.85:1	2.85:1	2.64:1
	2	1.89:1	2.02:1	2.02:1	1.75:1
	3	1.00:1	1.35:1	1.35:1	1.34:1
	4	—	1.00:1	1.00:1	1.00:1
	R	3.62:1	2.85:1	2.85:1	2.55:1
Clutch diam., in.		9.12	10.34	10.34	11.0
Axle ratios	S	2.73:1	3.08:1	3.08:1	3.73:1

		L-22 250	LG-3 305	LM-1 350	Z-28 350
Turbo Hydra-Matic transmission ratios	1	2.52:1	2.52:1	2.52:1	2.52:1
	2	1.52:1	1.52:1	1.52:1	1.52:1
	3	1.00:1	1.00:1	1.00:1	1.00:1
	R	1.93:1	1.93:1	1.93:1	1.93:1
Axle ratios	S	2.73:1	2.41:1	2.41:1	3.42:1
	E	—	—	—	—
	P	—	—	3.08:1	—

Note: No manual transmissions available in California for 1978.

1979 Camaro Engines

	CID	Config.	B&S, in.	Bhp @ rpm	Torque @ rpm	Compr. ratio	Carb.
L-22	250*	I-6	3.875 x 3.53	90 @ 3600*	175 @ 1600*	8.2:1	1V
L-22	250	I-6	3.875 x 3.53	115 @ 3800	200 @ 1600	8.0:1	1V
LG-3	305*	V-8	3.736 x 3.48	125 @ 3200*	235 @ 2000*	8.4:1	2V
LG-3	305	V-8	3.736 x 3.48	130 @ 3200	245 @ 2000	8.4:1	2V
LM-1	350*	V-8	4.00 x 3.48	165 @ 3800*	260 @ 2400*	8.2:1	4V
LM-1	350	V-8	4.00 x 3.48	170 @ 3800	270 @ 2400	8.2:1	4V
Z-28	350*	V-8	4.00 x 3.48	170 @ 4000*	265 @ 2400*	8.2:1	4V
Z-28	350	V-8	4.00 x 3.48	175 @ 4000	270 @ 2400	8.2:1	4V

*Asterisk denotes California and high-altitude ratings.

1979 Camaro Drivetrains

		L-22 250	LG-3 305	LM-1 350	Z-28 350
3- and 4-spd. manual transmission ratios	1	3.50:1	2.85:1	2.85:1	2.64:1
	2	1.89:1	2.02:1	2.02:1	1.75:1
	3	1.00:1	1.35:1	1.35:1	1.34:1
	4	—	1.00:1	1.00:1	1.00:1
	R	3.62:1	2.85:1	2.85:1	2.55:1
Clutch diam., in.		9.12	10.34	10.34	11.0
Axle ratios	S	2.56:1	3.08:1	3.08:1	3.73:1

		L-22 250	LG-3 305	LM-1 350	Z-28 350
Turbo Hydra-Matic transmission ratios	1	2.52:1	2.52:1	2.52:1	2.52:1
	2	1.52:1	1.52:1	1.52:1	1.52:1
	3	1.00:1	1.00:1	1.00:1	1.00:1
	R	1.93:1	1.93:1	1.93:1	1.93:1
Axle ratios	S	2.56:1	2.41:1	2.41:1	3.42:1
	E	—	—	3.08:1	—
	P	—	—	3.08:1	—

Note: No manual transmissions available in California for 1979.